YOU ARE WHAT YOU THINK

YOU ARE WHAT YOU THINK

BY DOUG HOOPER

VOL. I

Design and typesetting by Whatever Publishing
158 E. Blithedale, Suite 4
Mill Valley, Calif. 94941

Cover design by Dean Campbell

First Printing

ISBN 0-9604702-0-4

This book is dedicated to Eileen, who has been my wife for 44 years. Without her encouragement and help it would not have been written.

Preface

The distance between where you are now and where you aspire to be may seem so great you can not imagine ever reaching your destination.

However, in one respect there is little difference between imagination and reality. Whatever one is able to imagine does exist, if only on the mental plane. Once this happens, the first step has been taken to make your desire a reality.

I formerly wondered why a few were able to rise from obscurity to stardom or greatness while the majority remained glued to their present circumstances as if destined to remain there indefinitely.

After many years of conducting classes in prisons, and from thousands of letters I have received because of my newspaper columns, I believe I have found the answer. Those who broke through the boundaries of their present circumstances did so in their imagination first.

Just as a structure is erected in accordance with the plan of the architect, so is one's life a result of the mental image he holds firmly in his mind.

You are the architect in the process of building your life. This book will show you how.

Contents

1

Opening Up New Vistas

Many people are bored with life, and discouraged. Before they can escape from this boredom and discouragement they would have to be able to envision the probabilities of a more enriching life in the future. Unfortunately, however, they are living within an invisible circle, and this circle has become their personal boundary.

As time goes by, this circle will continue to grow smaller unless something is done to expand it. The probabilities of a change for the better will continue to diminish, at least in their own minds.

For example, if you are a salesman or a secretary, you do not think of yourself as being a lecturer or an artist. You accept what you are as a foregone conclusion, and the chances of your turning your life to a different direction are small. You will forever remain within that invisible circle, even though it is strictly of your own creation. The image you have inadvertently formed of yourself will prevent you from expanding your horizons.

Those who are considered successful had choices to make just as you have had during your life. There are always different avenues open to you so you are constantly forced to make decisions. You must realize that when you choose to do nothing that is also a decision.

If you are in a rut and can't get out of it, your mind first must be opened up to the fact that there are activities open to you other than those in which you are now engaged.

This can be done in the following manner: Think carefully about any abilities you possess, including those which have never been developed. Don't omit anything in which you were even slightly interested. You may have forgotten that when you were in grammar school you had an aptitude for drawing, for instance.

Make as long a list of your former interests as you can, and then make a conscious decision to develop some of them. Stop thinking of yourself as being limited to what you are now doing. Begin to envision some of the new possibilities that will open up for you.

This is the time to start using the power of your imagination. Without it you might not be motivated to continue. Right now, for example, you might find it hard to believe that you could ever advance very far in whatever direction you decide to go. Every advance you make, however small, opens up other possibilities. Those in turn will lead to still others.

Therefore, what might appear to be impossible to you at this point will become more and more probable as your talents are developed. In your imagination, do not place a limit on your achievements, but envision them as already accomplished.

This will be necessary if you are to persevere. Recognize your power to choose your own destiny. After all, everything you have ever done was once only a probability, which you chose to change into a reality.

Let us assume that you have now decided to activate your latent talents. You can expect to run into some opposition from within your own mind. For years you have been conditioned to believe you were cast in a certain mold, which was unchangeable.

These beliefs you have long held have given you a self-image that you now wish to change.

It will be necessary for you to make a very determined effort to alter these false beliefs about yourself. Your success or failure will depend upon this.

You can choose to allow your mind to dwell upon past failures and the thought that perhaps it is too late to develop dormant talents. If so, you will always remain within your invisible circle.

On the other hand, you can concentrate upon the unlimited possibilities that lie before you, and the avenues of expression which will open up as you proceed one step at a time.

You may be allowing your mind to focus upon the negative aspects of your life, both past and present, which causes these aspects to appear larger until they are entirely out of proportion. Your thoughts are your own, and are of your own choosing.

When you say "I can" it at least leads to a new "maybe," a new vision, a new conception of what you can do and be.

2

Everything is Now
And We Are All One

There are two things, at least, of which I hope to have a better understanding.

The first is to gain a better conception of "now," or the present moment. I would like to be able to gain happiness out of each hour and each day, instead of somehow putting it off until next week, or next month, or next year.

I suppose even this is not quite as bad as what others do. Many people are constantly thinking about how happy they used to be compared to their present unhappiness.

One way to accomplish this, according to my present limited understanding, is to learn to change one's mental state, adapting it to conditions and circumstances as they arise. When life becomes hectic and events don't turn out as planned, it would be advantageous if one could attain a calm, peaceful attitude, and thus view these events from a detached viewpoint. It would be similar to observing them occur as if they were happening to someone else, but at the same time doing whatever is necessary without reaction.

I would like to be able to consider the present as part of the future, not separate from it, as I am inclined to do. I believe if we all were to do this we would find it easier to be happy, rather than forever "hoping" to be happy.

It is a great mistake to try to live in the future because we despise the present. Many advanced teachers tell us that we are exactly where we are now because we have lessons to learn. These lessons are necessary if we are to progress. Those who spend their time dreaming of the future will find that their present problems will never be solved.

If it were possible to view our entire life all at once, as if from an airplane looking down over the earth, we would be able to see how everything that happened to us was connected with other events and led to either pleasant or unpleasant results. (We would probably be surprised that those happenings which we deplored at the moment led to good for us in the future, which was certainly unforseen at the time.) If we could view our life from this perspective the least it would do would give us a realization of the importance of our present thoughts and actions.

If I can absorb the idea that it is always "now," and always will be, I know I will learn to gain more enjoyment from each moment. I won't be concerned about the future because I will understand it is only an extension of the now. One's future is made in the present.

The other understanding I hope to reach during the coming year is that I am not separate from any other person. This means that the words "better" or "worse," or "higher" or "lower" no longer exist in my vocabulary.

I hope they do not exist in yours, either.

I fully recognize that some are acting in a manner which I consider to be wrong, and doing things I would not consider doing. I also recognize the fact that if I were in the same position, environment, temperament, etc., I might well act in exactly the same manner. Since I am far from perfect, how can I condemn anyone? The one who says, "I am holier than thou" is guilty of spiritual pride, and is heading for a fall.

If there are conditions in our society for which I am ashamed, I contributed to them by permitting them to exist. Everything I do has some connection with some-one else, somewhere.

If we feel self-righteous and believe we are better or different from others we are forgetting that we are all cast from the same mold, and are all a part of the whole. This does not mean that we must not live our own lives. We cannot expect someone else to live it for us. In the final analysis I believe each of us will be held accountable for our own acts, so in this sense we must stand alone.

We can, however, help others along the way. An ancient Hindu proverb reads "Help thy brother's boat across and lo, thine own has reached the shore."

Look upon every day as the whole of life, not merely as a section; and enjoy and improve the present without wishing, through haste, to rush on to another.

3

The Greatest of Gifts

Do you feel you don't have much to give this Christmas, and are you depressed because of it?

It may be true that you have little to give in a material way. You probably have been conditioned to believe that the quality of your gifts depends solely upon the extent of your material wealth. Actually, nothing could be further from the truth.

The true meaning of Christmas is lost if those who have little money to buy gifts feel they are inadequate and failures.

There is a gift you can give someone, and it is among the finest of gifts, comparable to the gifts of forgiveness and love. As with these two, it is within the reach of everyone to give because it is absolutely free.

Give someone hope for a better life! Almost everyone wants a better life, but many have lost hope of ever achieving it. Without hope there is little chance they ever will achieve it.

Over 100 years ago a great teacher from India said this concerning the gifts one can give to another, and it is just as relevant today as it was then:

9

"There are four kinds of help which we can render our fellow beings. We may give food, clothes, or money to a needy man, but his need returns.

"Next we can help someone gain an education, and this will prove to be very beneficial.

"The third, and what many would consider to be the greatest gift of all, would be to save a person's life. But that person might still die tomorrow.

"The fourth, and by far the greatest gift one can give to others, is to change their thinking. When you change their thinking you save their souls, and they can make their own way in life."

Those without hope must change their thinking or forever remain hopeless. This involves first the developing of a new self-image. You can help them accomplish this by emphasizing their good points, and convincing them of their own worth.

Hope for a new life! This great gift costs nothing. All it requires is concern for your fellow beings.

I know from experience that many have lost hope completely. These are the ones who must be reached at the time of Christmas and the coming of the New Year.

The reason so many believe their case to be hopeless is they think that it requires help from the outside to get them out of their predicament, and they are certain that help is not forthcoming. They are probably right, to a certain extent. Outer conditions won't change until their inner conditions change.

Whenever people tell me their situation is hopeless, I am immediately reminded of the convict I wrote about some time ago. He was spending time in a "strip cell," which contains nothing except a hole in the floor. It was an extreme form of punishment that was used in the past for convicts considered incorrigible.

He said at this point he felt he had reached the bottom of the ladder of life and was entirely without hope. Somehow, the realization came to him that if a change were to take place for the better a change would have to take place within himself first.

He knew there was only one place and one time to start, and that was right now, and right where he was. The next time the guard came with his daily ration of bread and water he thanked him instead of growling at him. This became his general attitude, and gradually the attitudes of others changed toward him.

Several years went by, and although his sentence had read "life imprisonment without possibility of parole," he was finally released. That was several years ago, and he is still living peacefully and happily with his wife and children.

I've known many other cases almost as hopeless as this with equally happy endings. In each case, the person had no help in the beginning except someone to make him believe that there is always hope, and that a better life need not depend on outside influences.

Someone said, "Hope is like the sun, which, as we journey toward it, casts the shadow of our burden behind us."

4

Actions Become Habit

David hadn't always been a loser. On the
until he was about 15, he had all the earmarks o
ing a winner.

He came from a closely knit, loving far
grades were good; he was active in sports ar
ambition. He felt his prospects for the future w
lent, and he exuded confidence.

Twenty years later, as a long-termer, he w
his story to my group at San Quentin Prisor
been convicted three times for armed robbery,
dope, and various other crimes.

Occasionally I encourage the men to go l
their past to the beginning of their careers in crii
are willing to do so because they hope their s
help others before it is too late.

There is no reason for them to tell anythin
truth. No one else is present, and they know I have no
influence one way or the other.

The incident about David happened several years
ago, but it came to mind again recently as I was listening
to a discourse on the addictiveness of such factors as

drugs, liquor, and gambling.

As David told his story, I began to correlate it with many others I had heard over the years. Suddenly, as I put them all together, the question of physiological addiction and the stereotyped reasons for a person's "downfall" seemed less important.

Much more important, I concluded, was how much a person's actions contribute to a change in his thought processes, and thus to a change in his consciousness and personality. These changes are the predominant factors in determining one's future.

This is David's story as he told it. I doubt that it is unusual.

His best friend, a star athlete, began smoking marijuana. At first, David was shocked, but it wasn't long before his friend encouraged him to experiment. Here is what happened as a result, in his own words, as nearly as I can remember:

"After I had been a user for a while, a change came over me. It was very gradual, and I probably was not aware of it at the time. I became less interested and less involved in school and sports. My grades, in which I had taken great pride, now lacked significance. Thoughts for the future and the ambitions I had fostered and nurtured, faded away. Most of my attention focused on the next 'joint,' and just about everything else became of secondary importance.

"As I look back in retrospect, I was not physically addicted at this point." (This, to my mind, is very important.) "What actually happened was that my thinking changed. If it's true, as I've finally become convinced after all these years, that what we think about is important, that was the beginning of the end as far as I was concerned.

"As the quality of my thoughts changed, my friends drifted away, and I found myself in an entirely different environment. I guess it was the Law of Attraction you talk about. Things that formerly had been abhorrent to me became a natural way of life.

"When some of my new friends reverted to crime to support their habits, it was easy and natural for me to drift along with them. By this time, although I may not as yet have been addicted, my consciousness and personality had changed to the extent I no longer had the will to resist. It wasn't long before I was on harder drugs, and the rest is history."

Others followed David with similar stories, different only in that for some the cause was liquor or gambling instead of drugs.

If you allow your mind to dwell on something for any length of time you will create a desire for it. This is true whether it is for your good or for your detriment. It works equally well either way. As Ralph Waldo Emerson, the 19th Century essayist and poet, said, "People become what they think about most of the time."

Anything we do with consistency eventually will become a habit, whether it is physically addictive or not. Before the habit is formed, a gradual change takes place in the consciousness of the person as a result of a change in the thinking habits. This results in a personality change and, in my opinion, is a large factor in transforming a positive life into a negative life.

All who were present that day at San Quentin agreed on one important point: Once they got into drugs, liquor, or gambling, their thoughts began to flow in a different direction. When this happened, their lives began to go downhill, and obviously they never stopped.

5

Take A Positive Look At the Past

Many people sell themselves short when they think of the past. Their minds focus much more on their failures than on their successes.

Unfortunately, this has a profound effect on their present life and consequently their future.

When you constantly look into the past for the cause of your unhappiness you will find that you are only looking for the negative features. This brings up a point I have often wondered about. We are forever looking for reasons why people are unhappy. Why don't we try to find out what makes happy people happy?

Looking for and dwelling upon all the reasons for your unhappiness can be dangerous, because you are forming habit patterns of thought which will be hard to break. This manner of thinking can easily prevent you from achieving your goals. You will become the type of person who will not attract positive people or events to you.

You can prove the logic and importance of this to yourself in the following manner. Recall to your mind an incident from your past in which you were highly successful and which caused you to be self-satisfied. It makes no difference how far in the past you have to go. You might have been a small child.

The main thing is to attempt to recapture that warm glow of feeling you experienced at the time.

You will be able to retain this pleasant feeling as long as you allow your mind to linger over the incident to the exclusion of other thoughts.

Now, compare the way you feel in contrast to the way you felt when you were thinking about your failures. You have taken your first step in the reconstruction of your past, because you are now looking upon it with a different perspective. Your past hasn't changed, but your way of thinking about it has changed.

As long as you persist in looking for past failures as the causes of your current problems you are reinforcing your belief in the problems. One's consciousness, or you might say personality, is formed by his or her thoughts, feelings and beliefs. To a great extent it is your consciousness that determines the quality of the events of your life.

When you are "down" mentally because of the nature of your thoughts concerning your past, your life continues its downward spiral. If you are constantly thinking about past failures, it is difficult to be successful in the present.

It is quite possible that you have painted an untrue picture of yourself. You are very likely a much better person than you give yourself credit for being. The reason you are "down" on yourself so frequently is that you do not permit yourself the luxury of dwelling on your good points.

If you will practice the mental exercise mentioned

earlier your self-image is bound to grow. This is one certain way to improve your present life and insure a happier future.

When things are going well for us we don't usually attribute our good fortune to past actions we have performed. However, when things are not going well we will immediately delve into the past for the reasons, which of course are always of a negative nature.

For example, the person who believes he cannot speak well in public will go back into the past and find reasons to support his belief, which will convince him that he will always be a failure as a speaker. If he were to seek out incidents in which he was successful and full of confidence, he would eventually live up to this newly acquired belief about himself.

This same premise applies to the state of one's health. When we feel below par, we compare the symptoms with those we had during a previous illness. This leads us to believe we will soon have a recurrence of that illness. It would be far better to concentrate on all the times we felt well.

If you believe you are ill, or a failure, or lonely, you won't have any trouble finding reasons to support this belief. You have allowed the positive aspects of your past to become buried deep in your consciousness, all but forgotten. If you are suffering under any of these conditions, it is up to you to dig them up and begin to relate your present life to past successes instead of to past failures.

6

'Labels' Should Be Ignored

The most fortunate of people are those with "self-esteem." The dictionary defines self-esteem as "A favorable opinion of oneself, conceit." I do not agree with the definition "conceit." One need not be conceited to have a favorable opinion of himself.

On the contrary, the person with self-esteem will not be anxious about himself and will thus be able to turn his attention upon those things which will be of benefit to himself and others. The conceited person usually acts in a manner to attract attention and has little confidence in himself.

Unfortunately, self-esteem is difficult to obtain. From my experience with people, it is relatively rare. This may be because we come into the world already "labeled," at least to a certain degree. We are not permitted to start out in life strictly as "ourselves."

The family we are born into already has a certain standing in the community. Consciously or unconsciously, we are expected by others to conform to that standard, whether it is high or low.

Two examples of this would be the child who is born

18

into a family where the father has a high professional position, or one who owns a successful business. If the child shows little or no interest in following in his father's footsteps, he is often made to feel guilty. This may result in his or her feeling worthless.

On the opposite end is the child born to a family where one or both parents have been in trouble with the law. Acts that would be passed off as childish pranks if committed by other children are attributed to heredity. The label which is placed upon the boy or girl as being a "bad" person following in his or her parents' footsteps becomes accepted by the child as being inevitable. Any chances of the child's developing a positive self-image is lost, probably forever.

Children born into "minority" families, either racially or religiously, face the problem of "fitting in" in their particular community. Although they may be superior in many ways to their neighbors, every effort will probably be made to cause them to feel inferior, or "out of it." They may find themselves responding to the beliefs held by others concerning themselves, even though the beliefs are false.

It is sad that many are given a disparaging label before they have a chance to get started in life. What can be done for those who are in one of these or other similar categories, and who suffer from a lack of self-esteem?

Perhaps nothing can be done *for* them, but there is something they can do for themselves.

First, they must recognize the fact that most of the opinions they hold about themselves were originally imposed upon them by others, and so are not necessarily true. They do not have to be bound by them, or accept them.

Then they must take steps to deliberately change the

opinions and beliefs they hold concerning themselves. This is not difficult. It does, however, require a rigid disciplining of the mind.

One's thoughts must be controlled to the extent that the person is able to direct his attention away from the negative aspects of his or her early childhood. No matter how strongly the belief that he belongs in the built-in category in which he was involuntarily placed, this concept must be regarded as false and must be overcome. Then, as mentioned previously, the mind should be focused solely upon past successes, even though they may have been small.

The only reason to mentally review a past failure is to extract a lesson from it. Once this is accomplished, the person will have a much more optimistic view of the future.

As an example, examine your own beliefs regarding the passing of the years. You will probably agree that they conform to almost everyone's opinion concerning the subject of one's growing old. The gradual slowing down and the loss of physical prowess, the increased likelihood of becoming ill, and of being lonely and not needed are taken for granted.

You do not have to accept these opinions, nor are you bound by others' opinions or beliefs about yourself. These opinions may have had a profound influence upon your past, but the future is in your hands!

Having a good year, you believe, is dependent upon many things. This is not true. Your having a good year is dependent mainly upon your changing your patterns of thought concerning yourself.

7

How to Get Out of a 'Rut'

If you believe you are in a rut, it is literally true. Years of habitual thinking along negative lines have caused "grooves" or "ruts" to form in your brain.

You may have a sincere desire to channel your thoughts along more positive lines but find it extremely difficult, if not impossible. Your thoughts automatically revert to following the old paths.

There is a method which, if practiced, will take you out of the rut and help you create desired changes in your life. Some call it the Law of Correspondence. It is not to be confused with the word "correspondence," which means communicating with someone by letter or other means. It is the correspondence defined as follows: "Relation of similarity, agreement."

This law makes it possible to change undesirable conditions and enables you to actually become the person you would like to be. All it requires is a certain amount of mind-control, and a sincere desire to succeed.

This is the method to be used: Decide what changes you wish in your life, or in yourself. Before you proceed further, be sure that these new conditions will be beneficial not only for you but also for all concerned. Now develop a habitual mental attitude that will "correspond" to the new circumstances you have chosen for yourself. Many will experience difficulty with this, being unable to form an attitude which is entirely foreign to their current status.

If this seems impractical to you examine your present circumstances from an objective viewpoint. Do they not conform to your mental attitude concerning them? What about your finances? Do you feel trapped and believe there is no chance for improvement? If so, your financial condition is only conforming to your beliefs concerning it.

Do the same with all the other important areas of your life: Your job, health, marriage, and so on. You will probably agree that they all conform to your prevailing mental attitude. It should become apparent to you that before the areas of your life which are unsatisfactory can improve, your mental attitude toward them must change first.

To some it will seem like "putting the cart before the horse." Your beliefs must correspond with the new, improved conditions in your life, which admittedly have not yet arrived. Therefore, a physical manifestation of faith may be required. Let us assume you are concerned about your finances. To prove to yourself that you believe they are improving, spend a little bit more for an article than you ordinarily would. It need be only a few pennies more. Occasionally have a more expensive lunch than is customary. This will serve to fortify your newfound belief in your prosperity.

Perhaps you are unhappy in your job. If so, this is an ideal area in which to utilize this law to advantage. You will find your working conditions will change for the better the same day you form mental attitudes toward your job to correspond to those you would have if you were happy in it. This is understandable if for no other reason than one does better work when happy in his job.

There is nothing new to this method of self-improvement. It will work for everyone who can get rid of the belief in limitation. Don't make the mistake of wondering how these improvements in your life will come about. Have faith that life must conform to the attitude you hold concerning it, and then be prepared to act.

New experiences do not come from looking backward, but from looking forward and upward.

8

The Game of Life is Not Over Until the Final Out

There is a certain similarity between a game of baseball and a person's life. The final result of a baseball game is never determined until the last batter is out in the last inning, no matter how far behind a team might be.

It is the same with life. No matter how much of a loser a person appears to be, as long as he or she is alive there is a chance to come back.

For this reason, I prefer baseball to those sports where time is a factor. A recent Super Bowl game was an example. With Dallas 17 points ahead, the last few minutes of the game were completely devoid of drama. There simply was not enough time for Denver to score three times while holding Dallas scoreless.

Contrast this to a World Series baseball game which took place in Chicago years ago. Chicago was leading Philadelphia 8 to 0 late in the game. Fans started heading for the exits because the game was so one-sided, but Philadelphia scored 10 runs in one inning and won the game, 10 to 8.

I formerly believed that peoples' lives could be

judged by their present status, and that the results were a foregone conclusion. For example, if a person reached middle age without accomplishing anything of note, it seemed reasonable to assume that the remaining years would be equally futile. The person who had drifted in and out of prison, or became a habitual drunkard, certainly did not appear headed toward a fruitful life. I no longer believe this way.

Many a drunkard has risen from the gutter and gone on to great accomplishments, and I have known so many "hopeless" convicts who are now leading productive lives I now accept such changes as a matter of course.

I was prompted to write this chapter because of an article that appeared in the January 1978 issue of Readers Digest. It is titled, "Don't Let Them Take Me Back!"

The article begins by stating that 15 years ago kids 17 and under committed less than 20 percent of serious crimes. Today, the figure is closer to 45 percent. While psychologists, police officials and juvenile authorities debate what should be done, a new experiment in a prison in Rahway, New Jersey, has stopped many young offenders in their tracks. Ironically, the idea came from a 35-year-old prisoner currently serving two life sentences.

This convict received word that his 12-year-old son was getting into trouble with the law. He felt that if his son, and other children, could get a glimpse of what prison life was really like, it might act as a deterrent. (Many times as I have entered deep into San Quentin and Folsom prisons I have thought along the same lines.)

The convict, Richard Rowe, was able to sell his idea to the proper authorities. As a result, about a year ago, nine boys, aged 12 to 17, were escorted into the prison. It was the first time minors had been allowed inside a maximum security prison. Although cocky and joking at first, their attitude soon changed to one of fear and horror.

After passing through several gates, they were led into a room where they were confronted by eight of the toughest men in the prison system, all lifers. For an hour and a half, these men painted a true picture of what prison is really like, not as it sometimes appears to be in the movies or television. It was a sober group of boys who left that day.

Since then, the idea has grown to where now, twice a day, five days a week, a group of youngsters is admitted to the prison. Of the first 3,200 boys and girls between the ages of 8 and 20 who have taken the "Rahway Course," only 6 percent have been in trouble since, instead of the expected 70 percent. This idea will probably spread throughout the country.

My purpose is not only to call attention to this program but to point out that Rowe and other "losers" taking part are being responsible for preventing thousands of youngsters from following in their footsteps.

These men are the dregs of society, and have admittedly committed heinous crimes. Despite the fact they could justifiably have been regarded as failures going nowhere, it is obvious their lives now have a meaning after all.

Perhaps they will fare better on Judgment Day than many of the rest of us! A person's life cannot be truly judged until he or she makes the final exit.

9

Throw Away the Crutches

There are any number of classes, group sessions, seminars, etc., that those looking for improvement in their lives may attend. I am sure all, or at least most, have something worthwhile to offer.

They all have one drawback, however, and this is no fault of theirs but of the individual doing the seeking. They tend to become a crutch, and may prevent the person from doing that which is necessary to do for himself before seeking assistance. As a consequence, those who need to do the most for themselves do the least, relying on outside influences to insure their happiness and well-being.

If you sincerely desire a happy, fulfilling life, a certain amount of groundwork should be laid first. Otherwise, although some progress will be made, it may be short-lived. When the sessions are over and contact with the class and teacher ceases, the aspirant soon slips back into the old ways. There was no solid foundation to build upon, which is necessary if the teacher's efforts are to have a lasting effect.

The ancient teachers were well aware of this. Before accepting a student, the teacher insisted that the student prepare his mind first with rigid disciplines and concentration exercises. Only when this was done to the teacher's satisfaction and the proper foundation was laid was the student accepted.

Before seeking assistance, I suggest you ask yourself this question, "What can I do to improve conditions in my life solely by my own efforts?" I think you will have to admit that you could make some improvement strictly on your own.

As an example, let us assume that loneliness is one of your problems. You would like to have friends as others do but don't know how to go about making them. Your first step should be to decide to become a more interesting person to be around. Analyze the quality of your conversation. You will probably discover that it mainly revolves around yourself and your problems. Also, that it is repetitious.

Determine to avoid the use of the word "I" as much as possible. Focus your attention upon the person with whom you are talking. If you train yourself to become a good listener you will soon be the most popular member of any group. Don't you think the most of the one who listens to and sympathizes with you?

You might wish to join in conversations but feel you have nothing to offer of interest. If this is the case, look for stimulating topics in magazines, or find interesting current events in newspapers to discuss. Become a self-made expert on some topic you believe would excite the curiosity of others. This will enhance your self image, which is no doubt currently at a low ebb.

It is your self-image which determines what you will expect from life. Therefore, to a large extent, it determines what you will receive. No matter what comes to you, you won't think you deserve it if you have a poor self image, and so will eventually lose it.

Don't allow your mind to dwell upon past failures. Place your entire attention upon reaching the goal you have set for yourself. You can be a pleasant person to be around, but not if your major concern is your own misery.

No matter what the real or imagined reasons for your self-dissatisfaction and unhappiness, don't seek help from others until you have done everything possible to improve conditions solely by your own efforts. You then will be much more receptive, and the things you learn will stand a much better chance of becoming a permanent part of your nature.

You may have unconsciously built a fence around yourself that is limiting you. Even though this fence exists only in your imagination, it is very real and can be removed only by you.

Unless you change inwardly, which means changing your inner thoughts and attitudes, no teacher or class can be of permanent help. However, if you decide to put forth some effort, teachers and classes can make your journey infinitely easier.

We all can put to good use the knowledge and help of others, but for the help to be effective we must also help ourselves. Don't become impatient and set unrealistic goals in the beginning. "The person who moved mountains began by carrying away small stones."

10

Discard Limiting Beliefs; Use Untapped Resources

There is quite a difference between belief and faith.

It is possible to believe in a project, for example, and not have enough faith to begin it. It is even possible to believe in yourself but not have enough faith to attempt to do the things you believe you are capable of doing.

The following anecdote will ilustrate this. A famous aerialist, nearing the end of his career, wanted to do something spectacular before retiring. He arranged to walk across Niagara Falls on a tightrope.

There was much advance publicity, and a great crowd lined the banks when the day arrived. There was tremendous excitement as he took his balancing pole and made his way slowly across the falls with the turbulent water beneath. When he reached the other side a huge roar of admiration went up.

The aerialist acknowledged the cheers of the crowd and then brought a small wheelbarrow onto the platform. He announced that he was now going back to the other side pushing the wheelbarrow with a man in it.

"Do you believe I can do it?" he called out.

"Yes," roared back the crowd.

He then singled out a man standing below.

"Do you believe I can do it?" he asked.

"Yes," shouted back the man, waving enthusiastically.

"Great, then you're first," answered the aerialist. The man fainted!

Scientists agree that hardly anyone uses more than 10 percent of his brain. We have heard and read this so often that we probably believe it, yet we do nothing about tapping the remaining 90 percent. If we had faith that we had so much untapped resources we would not hesitate to attempt those things we now consider to be beyond our normal abilities.

Your life is governed by your beliefs. No matter how well you feel now, you have been conditioned to believe that you will begin to deteriorate once you have reached a certain age. Therefore you believe it is too late to take on new projects or activities because there is no longer enough time remaining to you.

"It would be useless to start to learn to paint now," you tell yourself, "I should have started years ago."

Suppose Grandma Moses had so little faith in herself? She was 72 years old when she first began to paint.

Many of the beliefs you are holding onto concerning yourself are false. For the person seeking a more fulfilling life at any age there is only one alternative. All false beliefs must be rejected and replaced, especially those regarding your limitations. Until this is done, you will never begin to tap the great unrealized potential of the unused 90 percent of your mind.

Being excited and enthusiastic about life is not dependent upon being young in years. You can be eager to try new things, meet new people, explore new places, study a foreign language, and your chronological age is immaterial. Many young people are fatalistic, and believe there is nothing to look forward to. They are probably right, so long as they believe this way. It is far better to be "old" and optimistic than young and pessimistic.

One of the surest ways to become prematurely old is to believe you are no longer needed. It will cause you to become withdrawn and self-centered. You will find your interest in life waning, and your physical activities will decrease. As a result, your health will suffer. Your life will lack the meaning it must have if you are to feel fulfilled.

Believing you are not needed is one of the most destructive of the false beliefs so many hold concerning themselves. Everyone is needed somewhere and by someone. Everyone has something to give, even if it is only a word of cheer and an offer to be of assistance in some minor way.

There is an old saying that is very true. "It is impossible to help another without also helping yourself." An ancient Hindu proverb says: "Help thy brother's boat across and, lo, thine own has reached the shore."

Making yourself needed will help you avoid one of the saddest traps one can fall into with advancing years — self-pity. Belief in yourself and faith that God has given you many talents you have never used should give you the impetus you need.

Thus it will be impossible for you to feel sorry for yourself — you will be too busy.

11

Be A Good Winner or Loser

One of the most important decisions children are called upon to make is whether or not to participate in competitive sports.

Unfortunately, their decision is not always based upon their own wants or preferences; it may be literally forced upon them by pressures from peers and/or parents. I believe children should be permitted to feel "all right" about themselves if they prefer not to participate.

For many, being a member of a team is a very happy period of childhood. For others, however, it can be a very traumatic period. For example, when one is a member of a team it follows that he is responsible to a certain extent for its success or failure. Sooner or later there will come a time when he won't perform well and may be the cause of the team's losing.

This could lead to criticism from his teammates and coaches and, even worse, will probably lead to self-criticism. If the players and coaches cannot accept that the main purpose of adolescent sports is to have fun and to learn to be a good competitor, everyone loses in the long run.

Many lessons one learns in competitive sports are applicable to daily living. One is that we should accept the good days with the bad and not overreact to either. When this is done, the child's enjoyment of participation will be assured.

Some time ago, one of my grandsons decided to try out for Little League baseball. Sensing his apprehension, I wrote him the following letter:

Dear David,

This will be your first experience as a member of a team in competitive sports. Perhaps these thoughts will enable you to enjoy playing instead of coming to dread it, as many eventually do.

The best advice I can give you is this: Try not to be upset when you don't perform up to your own or others' expectations of you. You must realize that this happens to everyone at times.

Here is a suggestion that will prove helpful. Determine to do your best at all times. (If you do this and still perform below expectations you should not become upset, because you will know you could not have done better.) No one who has ever lived was able to do better than his best.

Never berate yourself if you strike out or make an error, even if it should come at a crucial point in the game. You know (and surely your coaches and teammates know) that the greatest players in the game, even those who are paid huge sums of money, often make errors and strike out.

One of the greatest shortstops of his time, Roger Peckinpaugh, once made eight errors in a World Series! If you remember this, it will help you overcome fear of failure (which is often the cause of failure).

Here is another tip. It may seem foolish to you at first, but it is based upon a great principle and will work wonders for you in every area of your life. Each time you come to bat, think of yourself as being a great hitter. Imagine how you would feel if you had already hit a couple of home runs off the pitcher, and then try to attain that feeling. Even if you have gone hitless for the last several times at bat, act out the part of a great hitter in your mind. Expect to get a hit every time you go to bat!

When you think about an upcoming game, always think of yourself as doing well. See yourself getting hits and making good plays in the field. Never visualize yourself as doing poorly. This applies to everything you do, not only in sports. You will be surprised how your body will act out the things you have previously pictured in your mind.

If someone on your team plays badly, encourage him instead of criticizing him. Some kids are not as good players as others, and your teammate feels unhappy enough without everyone calling attention to his shortcomings. When others criticize him, you be the one who always has a kind word.

As time goes by, you can learn to apply these principles to your daily life. For example, doing your best in whatever you do will give you an inner confidence, and you will be able to keep your emotions under control.

Regardless of how well or how poorly you play, you are a fine boy, and we are very proud of you. Your worth as a person does not depend upon your performance on the field. It depends much more upon your being a good winner or a good loser, whichever the case may be.

Love, Grandpa

12

We Attract That Which We Fear

Occasionally you will run across someone you once knew but haven't seen for a long time. Usually the person is the way you remembered him or her.

Most people retain the same basic characteristics they always had. Therefore, when you do meet someone from the past who apparently has undergone a complete metamorphosis it is a surprise.

Often the change is not for the better. Some of those you would least expect to do so have drifted into alcoholism, drug addiction, or compulsive gambling. Others, who did not appear to be going very far when you knew them, are enjoying a large measure of success. In either case, you wonder what took place in the intervening years to cause such changes.

The most obvious explanation would be to attribute the change to a particular incident which could be classified as either good or bad fortune, or luck. For example, you might say, "I can understand his taking to drink to drown his troubles. Look at the financial reverses he suffered through no fault of his own." Or you might point to a successful person and attribute his good fortune to the fact that he inherited a large sum of money,

37

which gave him his start.

At first glance, explanations such as these seem valid enough. However, how do you account for those who underwent similar experiences with entirely different results? What about those who attribute their success to an earlier adversity or those to whom the gift of a large sum of money has contributed to their downfall?

This situation stresses once again the tremendous truth, the understanding of which gives each of us control over our circumstances. As has been said, "It is not what happens to us but how we react to what happens that determines the result."

If the same occurrence causes different results in different people, it could not be the event itself that causes the changes; it is the person's reaction to the event.

One of the emotions we must guard against is fear, because fear can be extremely destructive. The person who, because of some adverse happening in his life, becomes fearful and beset by doubts concerning his ability to live a happy, productive life, actually changes inwardly. This inward change reflects in a subtle change in his outward experiences. He attracts to himself the things he fears.

Everyone has a certain "vibration" which is determined by his thoughts and mental reactions. Your vibration determines, to a great extent, what you will attract to yourself. If you experience a financial setback, you must choose the way this will influence your actions.

The longer you permit your thoughts to remain negative, the less your chances of pulling out of your financial dilemma. You will inadvertently send forth negative vibrations and so will continue to attract negative conditions. This cycle will continue until you make a conscious effort to change your thought patterns.

Many are going through an unhappy experience, such as a divorce, which may result in a period of depression. This is understandable, but so long as a person allows himself to remain in this mood, the Law of Attraction will prevent happy experiences from coming into his life. On the other hand, some persons emerge much stronger and happier because of the experience. The important point to remember is that it is you who must make the final decision as to what your reaction to any situation will be!

It is a mistake to give power to any person or situation to affect your life. It is not something you would do deliberately, but you do it without being conscious of what you are doing. By allowing your mind to dwell on your so-called misfortune, you are reinforcing your belief in its power to control your life.

One of the greatest revelations one can experience is that he has the capacity to overcome, and thus rise above, his difficulties.

13

Change Inner Attitudes

It is possible to remain contented even though causes for discontent remain in your life. You may find this hard to believe. You may have convinced yourself that until a particular problem is solved, or changes take place in a situation or person, you will remain unhappy. This need not be true.

Sometimes the harder one tries to solve a problem, the more difficult the problem is to overcome. Perhaps a better method of eliminating areas of dissatisfaction from our lives is to place our attention elsewhere. The mind is capable of only one thought at a time. So long as your thoughts are diverted from your problems, the problems will assume a lesser role in your life.

This is not meant to be an endorsement for "escapism." When one learns to control his mind to the extent that he can direct his thoughts where he wishes, he is able to place things in their proper perspective.

It is easy to become depressed and thus unable to function well if one's mind is constantly focused on the negative aspects of life. Try for a time to take your mind off your problems and place your attention upon something that has no relation to them.

Suppose, for example, you find yourself feeling very tense. You try to relax, but the more you concentrate on relaxing, the more tense you become. Forget about relaxing and focus your mind on a quiet place you once visited, or upon a past pleasant experience. Your tension will disappear without a conscious effort.

The more attention we give to a problem, the more important it becomes. Another example is the person who desperately wants to lose weight. His mind becomes consumed with thoughts of food — what he should or should not eat. Instead, he should devote his energy and thoughts to developing other interests or hobbies.

One's attention should be directed away from the problem; otherwise you are feeding it mentally. A desire that is never fed will eventually die a natural death.

It is foolish to give a person or situation the power to spoil your happiness. You must realize that you cannot always manipulate others to suit you, or force them to behave in a way you want them to behave, nor should you do so. As I have pointed out before, it is not the way a person acts that is upsetting you, it is that he is not acting as you think he should act.

If you have suffered a severe loss, it is only natural that your thoughts will dwell on this loss. Suppose you diverted your attention to what is left instead of thinking about what you lost. To repeat: You can entertain only one thought at a time. You will be much happier if you direct your thoughts along positive lines.

If you don't believe it is possible to be contented while there are problems in your life, try this: Think back on a time when you were in a happy mood, feeling contented, even though it was short-lived. Perhaps you were enjoying a movie or a television program. Some

41

persons find pleasure in a meditation period each day. Whatever your time of contentment, did not your problems still exist? Nevertheless, you were happy in spite of them.

During the short time your attention was placed elsewhere, your troubles were momentarily forgotten. Therefore, they lost their power to upset you. This does not mean that problems do not have to be faced. It does mean that you are better able to handle them because you can look at them more objectively.

When you realize that you can be happy in spite of adverse circumstances, you have experienced a taste of happiness that is of a permanent nature. Your happiness is not dependent upon overcoming your problems, but upon changing your inner attitudes. Now you are in control! It is possible, without changing anything on the outside, to be happy within yourself. This is a great discovery, because you will find it no longer necessary to solve your problems all at once.

You may find that all you need to do is remember these simple words, "Let go, and let God."

14

Letters Affirm Value of Teachings

It is usually much easier to solve other people's problems than your own. I suppose that is because you can view their problems more objectively. Also, it is simple to advise, "Don't do as I do, do as I say."

Nevertheless, many problems can be solved if you have an objective viewpoint toward them. It is the recognition that we can choose how much power we wish to allocate to the problem that makes the difference. With this recognition comes a feeling of control, instead of the feeling of being a victim.

This is not meant to imply that if a very definite problem exists in your life it should be ignored or deliberately avoided, only to be faced at some later date.

It does imply that no matter what the problem, it can be at least partially solved or eased by a change of attitude on your part. It is not totally dependent upon the person or the situation changing.

Of all the books I took to the prisons to give to the men over the years, there is one that probably had more impact upon them than any other. I gave away hundreds, and they only cost 15 cents each! It was written by

43

James Allen and it was called "As a Man Thinketh." Here is a paragraph from this wonderful little booklet, which is still in print.

> *A man will find that as he alters his thoughts toward things and other people, things and other people will alter toward him. Let a man radically alter his thoughts, and he will be astonished at the rapid transformation it will effect in the material conditions of his life. Men do not attract that which they want, but that which they are. The divinity that shapes our ends is in ourselves. All that a man achieves is the direct result of his own thoughts. A man can only rise, conquer and achieve by lifting up his thoughts. He can only remain weak and abject and miserable by refusing to lift up his thoughts.*

Throughout history great teachers have been trying to tell us of our inner power to control our circumstances simply by learning to control our thoughts and attitudes. "Be therefore transformed by the renewing of your mind," the Bible tells us.

Harvard professor Dr. William James said, "Much of what we call evil can often be converted into a bracing and tonic good by a simple change of the sufferer's inner attitude from one of fear to one of fight."

If you can convince someone with problems that he or she is not powerless to overcome them, or that no situation is unalterable even though outside help is not readily available, that person's battle is won.

Many of us, when confronted by a seemingly unsolvable problem, allow it to overwhelm us. Not being able to conceive of an early solution, we give up the fight.

We should recognize the fact that every problem has a solution, and that a solution may be dependent soley upon your own efforts and attitude toward it.

One effective approach is to try to live through one day at a time. Almost anything can be faced for 24 hours. It is strange how a different way of looking at things can change an apparently insurmountable obstacle into one that can be easily handled.

Two thousand years ago the great philosopher Epictetus made two observations that give great encouragement in time of trouble. His thoughts have been echoed many times both before and since.

"We ought to be more concerned about removing wrong thoughts from the mind," Epictetus said, "than about removing tumors and abscesses from the body."

Now, twenty centuries later, doctors are agreeing that many ailments can be traced back to mental maladjustments to life and its problems.

Another observation he made that has been repeated countless times was this: "It is not the events but our viewpoint toward the events that is the determining factor."

No one can, or should, take on another's burdens. Whenever possible, however, one can endeavor to ease those burdens by showing the person that the solution to his dilemma is within his own province.

As another great teacher said long ago: "The greatest help one human being can give another is to help him change his thinking, because when you help him change his thinking you save his soul, and he can then make his own way in life."

15

It Is Never Too Late

It may be difficult for many to believe that a new life is possible for them, but it is.

I have steadily maintained that there is a very thin line separating the person who is unhappy and considered a failure, and the one who is happy, well-adjusted and successful. This is despite the fact it is generally believed that many steps must be taken before a change in one's life can be effected.

I believe a new life begins the moment one learns that a change must first come from within himself. I have witnessed many examples first hand which support this belief. Occasionally I hear, "It's too late; the damage has been done." They are wrong. There is always time for a new start.

A few months ago I received a letter from a man who said he had not experienced a happy day for as long as he could remember. He asked if I could help him. I did not want to sound cruel, but I told him the truth. I said I could not help him but, fortunately, I knew the one person in the world who could — himself. I went on to

46

explain how he might begin, based on an age-old technique.

"Sit quietly until your mind is cleared of all extraneous thoughts and you can view your situation objectively," I advised him. "Examine the nature of your predominant daily thoughts and you will probably find that they are, for the most part, focused on yourself and your problems. If this is true, you are automatically eliminating many sources of enjoyment from your life. You are not even aware that sources of enjoyment might exist for you.

"At first, you will find it hard to take your mind off yourself and your problems, but don't become discouraged. You must face the fact that you have become self-centered, and it will take a conscious effort on your part to change. The reward, however, will more than compensate for your efforts.

"There are simple steps you can take which will help you accomplish this. For example, you will find that if you look casually at a flower it will give you little pleasure. Now concentrate upon it and you will begin to derive enjoyment from its beauty, perhaps, or its scent. It is this giving of attention that leads to appreciation and enjoyment. If you give an object your undivided attention it will 'take you out of yourself completely.' Next, transfer your attention to other people, and learn to feel concern for them. You will never find happiness by living a selfish or self-centered life. Happiness lies in forgetting the self and through enjoying and understanding the life in people and nature. When you are forgetful of yourself, you will find yourself drawn into the lives of others."

The man told me later that by learning to focus his

attention upon objects of nature, and finding beauty which he had never noticed before, he had less time to indulge in self-pity.

Then he gradually transferred this concentrated attention to those with whom he came in contact. He began to feel a genuine concern for them, which of course resulted in their feeling concern for him. He could scarcely believe the changes that had taken place in his life in such a short time, and he had accomplished it by himself!

His experience proves once again my original assumption. In this particular case, he crossed the line between happiness and despair by first transferring his attention to objects of nature. Then, after his mind had become conditioned, he learned to transfer his attention to other people.

Some cross this imaginary line by concentrating upon thoughts of love instead of hate and resentment. Others do it by deliberately discarding all negative thoughts of themselves and of others. The method used is not important. It is important to know that it is never too late for a fresh start, or a new beginning.

16

Is Life Dull and Depressing?

If your life is dull and you find yourself bored and depressed, there is one sure antidote — do something different.

It is easy to get into a rut but difficult to get out. Even pleasurable activities can become boring when allowed to become too routine. The golfer who plays every Saturday morning might enjoy it more if he changed to some other form of recreation occasionally.

When one loses the ability to be spontaneous and allows himself to become set in his ways, life is no longer fun. You have no way of knowing what you can do if you never try anything different.

You may have to spend a little more than you think you can afford, but that can be advantageous too. It is good to break away from a set routine even if it sometimes means straining the budget. Money has a way of being attracted to those who are not too attached to it and repelled by those who are.

Perhaps you have been concentrating on your limitations rather than upon your abundance. If you develop faith and confidence that you earn enough to supply your needs and desires, you will earn enough. It is you who put the limits on yourself.

Try a new restaurant, even if it is expensive. Purchase tickets to a musical or a play, if this is out of your normal pattern. Go to a museum or attend a class, even though you think you might not be interested. It will not only prove beneficial but it also will result in your making new friends.

If a change should be forced upon you that you cannot avoid, be glad for it, even if it causes you to be fearful temporarily. You may find yourself in a strange situation, not of your own choosing, and you may not be sure that you can handle it. You can take heart in the fact that some of our greatest minds tell us that, without exception, we are capable of handling whatever challenges life has to offer. Otherwise, we would not have been given the challenge.

Many people regard their jobs as nothing more than a means of filling time or making a living. If this is true in your case, try doing your work a little bit better. This effort will not only serve to make it more interesting but also will inevitably lead to a better job!

Once you start using your imagination and release yourself from a set way of doing things, your accomplishments will surprise you.

A change in one's marital status can be traumatic, but it can also force you to use talents you were never conscious of possessing. The "Law of Compensation" works in strange ways.

It is important to realize that it is not necessary to wait for something to happen to bring yourself out of a set routine. You can deliberately initiate the change yourself.

50

You may literally have to shock yourself into action. Finnish health addicts believe in going from a hot sauna into ice-cold water. If you think about it first you won't do it, but if you do it you will feel wonderful. Once you expose yourself to the excitement of doing something a bit different, you will find the possibilities are endless.

Marriages sometimes deteriorate when one or both partners become too set in their ways. The very characteristics that attracted them to each other in the first place now no longer exist. This problem can be remedied quickly by the use of a little imagination.

Do some of the things you used to have fun doing when you were dating. They may seem foolish to you now, but do them anyway. You will both be pleasantly surprised when you rediscover the excitement you felt when doing "foolish" things together.

The "Family Word Finder" explains the origin of the word "rut." It comes from the word "route." It is a track — as worn by a wheel, or a settled routine. Thus in the old days one could follow the route to the next town, or follow the rut, and it would be the same.

Some people are happiest when staying in the rut, or following the same routine day after day. If so, there is little reason to change. However, doing so may prevent you from discovering all life has to offer. Occasionally take a different "route" and do something out of the ordinary. To start, all you need to do is to change your patterns of thought.

17

Don't Let the World Go By

Inertia is a great deterrent to progress. In fact, unless something moves — including yourself — it will forever remain stationary.

The quality of our lives is not only determined by what we do, but by what we do *not* do. Basic principles and Natural Laws apply to the doer and the non-doer alike. If you don't begin something, nothing happens.

Some of our greatest thinkers, Emerson for one, discovered that "The act of doing actually generates the power within you to continue doing." He put it another way when he stated, "Do the thing and you will have the power."

If nothing exciting is happening in your life, it is easy to blame it upon some factor over which you maintain you have little or no control. The fact is you haven't done anything which would cause something exciting to happen!

You can't escape the Law of Cause and Effect. If you do certain things, you will receive certain results. If you do little or nothing, you can expect little or nothing in return. It is you who are the causative factor.

The mere act of your starting a project will go a long way toward furnishing you with the power needed to complete it. Generate enough energy and motivation to begin, and then rely on this power to keep you in motion. As long as you keep on, it becomes increasingly easier to continue, because you will build up momentum.

The reason you failed to complete projects or achieve goals in the past was that you allowed yourself to fall back upon your old ways of inertia, and so your forward movement stopped.

Think back over the last few years. What happened to the exercise program you began, the new study you undertook, or whatever it was you started and for some unaccountable reason discontinued.

Had you persevered just a little longer the chances are you would have gathered enough momentum to go on. Imagine what you would have accomplished by now had you done so!

Apparently, life expects us to take the first step. After that, it will cooperate, but it cannot help us if we give up. It is important to realize that if we persist we don't have to go it alone.

Frequently the Scriptures refer to a great spiritual force that is within us, but it is lying dormant until called upon. This means we do not have to rely on our "little selves" for accomplishment. When we do, we fail. When we believe in and call upon this "something extra" we succeed.

Sometimes a person's initial desire is not strong enough to motivate him to continue and complete what he starts. For example, a person sets a goal of a certain weight loss. He begins with enthusiasm, but soon finds he lacks the necessary will power to continue to discipline himself.

This is a crucial point, because now he will probably allow his imagination to take over. He will start thinking about the "goodies" he has been denying himself, and allowing his mind to dwell on them.

This is fatal because one's imagination will always prevail over one's will power. (The only recourse is to keep the mind focused on the desired result, not on the temptations you will face along the way.)

Whether it is a new project you wish to start, or some sort of self-improvement program, it is a form of self-expression. Self-expression is vital to one's happiness. Knowing that you are not realizing your potential causes you to be dissatisfied with yourself. The desire to express oneself is natural to everyone. Not satisfying this yearning results in a vague feeling of discontent which will remain until the urge is fulfilled.

Dr. Eric Fromm, whose writings have helped thousands, explains this desire for expression much better than I can. "Life has an inner dynamism of its own. It tends to grow, to be expressed, to be lived. It seems that if this tendency is thwarted, the energy directed toward life changes into energies directed toward destruction."

Reach for some of that untapped ability that is within you by using the power of your mind in a positive way. When you develop a negative conception of your possibilities you contribute to your own defeat.

18

Open Your Mind
To Reach Your Potential

A strange story came out of a hypnosis research laboratory in Stanford, Calif. It was reported in a newspaper article. I am repeating it not only because of its interesting content but also to illustrate a point. I would guess that at least one-half of those reading about it will reject it immediately, considering the idea too difficult to accept.

A man at the Stanford laboratory complained he no longer could use his right leg. It buckled and dragged when he walked. He was hypnotized and, while under hypnosis, he remembered that he had quarreled with his boss and wanted to kick him. He had to suppress the desire and subsequently lost the ability to use his right foot and leg. When he was awakened from hypnosis, his right foot and leg again worked normally.

I am not an authority on hypnosis, so I am unable to affirm the validity of the story. That is immaterial to the point I wish to make, which is this:

Whenever you hear of something which is beyond the range of your normal, everyday experiences, it does no harm to begin with the assumption that it is true. If you refuse to believe something simply because you

55

have never experienced it, you are definitely limiting your potential for growth.

If your outer world is a reflection of your beliefs about it, and I believe it is, then why limit your world by refusing to accept concepts because they are unfamiliar to you?

Contrast the person who is able to see the possibility of the Stanford story being true with the one who automatically rejects it. A new world opens up to the one who can believe. Old concepts — such as the belief that improvements in health or in life in general are not probable — are discarded. In this case, one realizes that perhaps his ailments were created by his own inner feelings that have been suppressed, and therefore a cure is possible.

It is the ability to keep an open mind that is important! Those who cannot see the likelihood of this and other similar stories being true are destined to remain prisoners in the little world they have created for themselves. They will accept whatever happens to them as being irrevocable. These are the ones who permit negative experiences from their past to affect their lives and rob them of their self-confidence.

On the other hand, those able to keep an open mind are never without hope. We did not start out in life with a mind full of self-doubt, fear, and pessimism. In its original state, our mind was free of these negative qualities. Therefore, if we have them now, they must have been acquired along the way.

If your mind is closed to everything beyond your present comprehension, it must be because you permitted yourself to be influenced by others who held this limited viewpoint. You don't have to remain this way, however. Anything acquired can be discarded.

To change your self-doubts into self-confidence, discard all negative opinions you hold concerning yourself and the possibilities life holds for you. Those negative opinions may be based upon false information. Visualize your mind as it was before it became permeated with these false conclusions.

When your mind is once again free from negative concepts you will become receptive. You won't automatically reject something as being impossible, just because it happens to be beyond your experience at the present.

Many live under the assumption that all they can see is all there is. Their lives are filled with frustration because they cannot imagine any way an improvement could take place. It is a matter of clinging to false assumptions instead of discarding them.

I once pointed out that just around the corner there may be a beautiful castle waiting for you to move into. If your mind remains closed to the possibility of its existence, however, you probably will never see it.

To appreciate and recognize the potential that you really have is one of the most important steps you can ever take.

19

Change Your Response to Improve Your Situation

If you ever enter Folsom State Prison, California's only maximum-security institution — and I hope you don't — you will first go through the main gate. There, you will be put through an electronic detector, and a stamp will be placed upon your wrist, which will be checked when you leave.

The distance between this gate and another, which leads to the inner confines of the prison, is approximately one-half mile. At this point the guard calls the guard at the main gate to double-check your identity.

A small van, driven by an inmate, serves as a taxi for prison personnel and outside teachers. It goes back and forth between the two gates all day long. On one of my monthly visits I happened to be the only passenger, and I asked Jim, the driver, how he liked his job.

"I can't stand it," he answered. "Back and forth all day long, with never a change of scenery."

Although Jim was not a member of the class I conducted in the prison, I decided to put one of the principles I teach to a test.

"You can make your job enjoyable without changing the route, the van, or the passengers," I told him.

"That sounds great," he said, with a tolerant smile. "Now tell me how to go about it."

I told him there are many people who find their jobs boring, but that situation can be changed.

"In your case," I said, "I suggest you start up a conversation whenever possible with your passengers."

"I've always wished I could do that," said Jim, with surprise, "but unfortunately I don't have anything of interest to talk about."

This is a complaint I frequently hear from those who find it difficult to carry on a conversation. But this problem can easily be overcome.

"You may not have anything to talk about, but the other person does," I told him. "Everyone loves to talk about himself."

I related a story I remembered reading about a famous man who sat next to a very boring person at a dinner party. The person, also a celebrity, talked about himself almost constantly throughout the dinner.

The other, because he was so bored, let his mind wander and scarcely said a word. In spite of his almost total silence, he later heard himself referred to by the loquacious one as the most brilliant conversationalist he had ever had the pleasure of meeting!

I suggested to Jim that he direct a question to each person who entered his cab. This question must relate directly to the person's life, his job, or his opinion on some matter. He said he would try.

The next month when I saw Jim again I was pleased to see that he looked happy and cheerful.

"Everyone thinks me brilliant now," he told me. "All I've done since I last saw you is ask questions, and yet people actually seek me out so they can talk to me. I ask, 'When did you first feel you were qualified for the type of work you are doing?' or, 'What is your opinion on this matter?' My job is not only more enjoyable now but I have become so popular I can hardly believe it."

The first lesson to be learned from Jim's experience is that in order to be considered a good conversationalist all one actually needs to do is ask questions and listen. However, there is another lesson that is even more important. We develop habitual responses to certain situations, and it is these responses that must be changed before an improvement in the situation can take place.

We have the power, if we wish to call upon it, to effect changes by responding or reacting in a different manner to those troublesome situations than we have done previously.

In Jim's case, we find his job did not change one iota. He still drove the same van back and forth the same number of times a day. The scenery remained the same, and his passengers were the same people they had always been. All that happened to effect this tremendous change in his life was his changed response to a situation he had formerly deplored.

What a wonderful feeling it is to learn we do not have to wait or pray for outside changes to take place in our lives in order for us to be happy! We look around at our world and take for granted it must ever remain the same.

Perhaps it does. That need not always be our concern. Our concern should be, "How can I make this situation more tolerable by responding differently to it?"

When this is accomplished, the situation, which once was unpleasant, becomes pleasant. The situation itself didn't change, however. The change in our reaction and our response is what did the work.

20

The Law of Correspondence

Those who watched the television program "Holocaust" will remember a statement made by one of the nazi officers. He addressed it to a German captain who, up to this point, had been reluctant to take part in the mass murders which were taking place.

He said, "Once you have killed one person it is easy to kill ten. When you have killed ten it is easy to kill a hundred, and when you have killed a hundred, you can kill a thousand."

As horrible as this sounds it is a classic example of a simple principle. This principle, as with all principles, can be applied for good as well as for evil.

I came across the following verse in a book on Yoga and mental development which was written about 80 years ago:

> Vice is a monster of so frightful mien
> That to be hated needs but to be seen.
> Yet seen too oft, familiar with her face,
> We first endure, then pity, then embrace.

In modern language, it means that when we think in a certain way for any length of time, we gradually become the sort of person who corresponds to the way we think.

The author of the book, Ramacharaka, used as an example a young person with very high scruples and ideals with no desire to be otherwise. When placed in a position where he is exposed to hearing or seeing those who lead a sensual life (such as those who use drugs and alcohol) he becomes curious. His mind begins to speculate on what it might be like.

If he allows his imagination to cultivate and nourish the thoughts long enough, the desire to experience will prove too much for him. Eventually, he will find himself doing the very things that were foreign to his nature a short time ago.

This accounts for the shock many parents experience. They cannot understand the changed behavior of their children, especially when it is so contrary to their early upbringing and training.

The principle is called the Law of Consistency or the Law of Correspondence. It is one of the most powerful life-changing principles when used in a positive way. It maintains that it is impossible to think, feel, and believe one way and act in another way for any length of time.

One's actions must correspond to, or be consistent with, one's inner feelings and beliefs. Otherwise either one's actions will change or one's inner feelings and beliefs will change.

Consider this, and accept it as a fact if you can. The way you act will eventually be determined by the way you think, feel, and believe. If this is true, then the reverse must also be true, and perhaps this is even more important. The way you think and feel about yourself will be determined by the way you act.

This fact should be encouraging to those who have attempted unsuccessfully to change their self-image by using will power. They have a sincere desire to improve the quality of their lives but soon give up. The negative feelings and beliefs they hold concerning themselves are too deeply ingrained in their consciousness, so they cease trying.

The opposite approach is easier. With will power and determination, one can act in a different manner than has been his habit. He then must change into the person who will correspond to or become consistent with his actions.

As an example, consider a person with little or no self-confidence. He dreads speaking before a group. His actions will be consistent with his beliefs about himself, and so he avoids all situations where he might be called upon to do so. Suppose he were to act differently and deliberately create situations in which he would be forced to perform, such as joining a Toastmaster's Club.

This new action would no longer be consistent with his previous beliefs about himself as one lacking confidence. If he continues to act in a positive manner he will gradually change inwardly so that his feelings and beliefs will correspond to his positive actions.

By acting in the manner in which a self-confident person would act, you cause your negative feeling about yourself to drop away on their own accord.

21

Refuse to Live in the Past

When something disturbing happens to us, it is understandable that we experience some negative reaction. It would be wonderful if we were able to control negative reactions, but most of us have not reached that point.

After the disturbing event has happened, however, the situation changes. One begins to have more of a choice as to how he will continue to react. The more time that elapses, the easier the choice should become.

After a period of time, one should be able to gain enough control to put the event in the proper perspective. He must now decide how long he wishes to give something that happened in the past the power to affect his happiness in the present. Many persons fail to recognize this power of choice and permit the unfortunate incident to continue to influence their lives. As a result, they are frustrated and unhappy much longer than is necessary.

Once you begin giving power to something that has already happened, the event seems to grow in importance, rather than diminish. For example, when you think back upon a time when you were embarrassed, the memory is usually more painful than the event was when it happened.

When you do something you consider wrong, you may feel slightly guilty. If you continue to relive the incident, the guilt you feel will be much more devastating. Far better to make restitution if possible and resolve not to repeat the act, then remove the incident from your mind.

The acts you committed which made you feel embarrassed or guilty are over. It is only your thoughts concerning them that cause the reaction to continue.

Someone does something that makes you feel angry. The more you think about it, the angrier you become. If you continue to dwell upon the incident, your anger will be more pronounced than it was in the beginning. If this keeps up, you are actually giving the person who made you angry control over your life! Once you accept the fact that overcoming your frustrations is dependent only upon the extent that you can control your own thoughts, you will be in charge of your life.

Allowing unhappy events to make your life miserable long after they have happened seems foolish, and yet this is what you do when you live in the past. It may be unrealistic to expect to be in complete control over what happens to you, but you can at least see the possibility of being able to control your thoughts about — and your reactions to — what happens.

I've noticed this about many people: When things are going badly, they blame this situation on something they have done or left undone and experience guilt feelings as a consequence. On the other hand, when things are going well, they attribute it to luck. If things are going well, why not give yourself credit for performing positive actions which cause good to come to you? After all, you blame yourself when they are not going well.

One should strive to develop faith and belief in himself and in his powers to control his life. If you try the following experiment for at least several days, it will give you an inkling of this power:

No matter how frustrated and unhappy you feel now, take the stand that life is for you and not against you. Stop expecting the worst and expect positive things to happen. If you practice this faithfully, subtle changes will occur almost immediately. (I have seen this happen so many times I know it is not accidental.)

The moment a person's attitude toward life changes, his circumstances must change. He emanates positive "nerve currents," or "vibrations," and no longer attracts negative situations and conditions. It has long been taught that the conditions we attract to us must coincide with our inner attitudes and beliefs.

Ralph Waldo Trine, author of *In Tune With the Infinite*, wrote: "As science is so abundantly demonstrating today, the things we see are but a very small fraction of the things that are. The real, vital forces at work in our lives and in the world about us are not seen by the ordinary physical eye. Yet they are the causes of which all things we see are merely the effects.

"Thoughts are forces; like builds like, and like attracts like. For one to govern his thinking, then, is to determine his life."

22

Discard False Concepts Concerning Yourself

According to those who have almost died, our entire life will parade before our eyes in the last few moments.

Most of us, I am sure, will have some regrets as we are forced to look back. However, we must remember to be fair with ourselves when our time comes. We may find that when viewed with the perspective of time, those parts of our life which we now believe we will view with regret will appear in a more favorable light to us.

No one remains the same. This is one of the great paradoxes of life. We may look back with astonishment, and perhaps even with remorse, that we could have done the things we will see ourselves doing, forgetting we were different persons then.

Hopefully, when the time comes to view our life from beginning to end, we will give ourselves a break. Perhaps we will have gained enough understanding to realize that we had the choice to make whatever we wished of our lives. If it becomes apparent that we sometimes made the wrong choice, it was only because at the time we did not know any better.

We will probably see, in retrospect, that many times when we experienced adversity it prepared us for the good that followed. Many worthwhile things that happen are preceded by adversity. If only we could realize this instead of having to wait for the passage of time to prove it to us.

It will be only natural when looking back over our lives to say we shouldn't have done this or that, or that we should have acted differently in a certain situation. Given the perspective of time, and the knowledge and wisdom that should accompany this perspective, perhaps we will be able to understand that everything that happened to us had a purpose.

If it did not always turn out for the best, at least it was our choice. No one forced us to do what we did, nor prevented us from doing what we did not do.

If it is true that we must review our life at the time of our death, we should take every opportunity now to make the viewing a pleasant one. You can make sure you will enjoy the last part of your life as it flashes by, even though the first part may not be entirely to your liking.

How would you like to have a box seat for the review of your life and be forced to contemplate the following? You see yourself failing in one undertaking after another because of some psychological barrier which existed only in your own mind.

You will observe, as you view the overall picture, how you were vulnerable to the opinions of others and how you allowed these opinions gradually to destroy your self-image.

You must look at all the opportunities you allowed to pass you by because you believed yourself inadequate. Imagine your dissappointment as you see all your unused potential go to waste. This will be especially true now when you realize what might have been.

Fortunately, this need not happen. There is still time to mold the picture to your liking and insure a pleasurable time as your entire life passes before your eyes. If this is to be accomplished, however, some drastic changes in your thinking and in your concept of yourself may be called for.

You might start now by refusing to accept anything concerning yourself as a foregone conclusion. You may already have decided that certain things in your life will never be available to you or that your abilities are limited. Your first move, if you are to make the viewing of your life review pleasant when the time comes, is to discard immediately those false concepts concerning yourself.

Unless you do this, you will pass up many opportunities. You are placing an invisible but very real circle around yourself and you will never emerge from it until you change your thinking.

As you are forced to review all the happenings and all the experiences of your life, you will undoubtedly find that you turned out to be exactly the person your mind told you that you were.

Change your mind now before it is too late.

23

'No Man Is An Island'

Everything we do has a direct effect on someone. Even those who consider themselves and their lives inconsequential are responsible for the happiness and well-being of many others.

If we were aware of this, perhaps we would choose our actions more carefully. We need to develop a sense of pride and a feeling of responsibility in our school, our friends, our family, and the company for which we work. Each of us is a part of the whole, and we should never expect it to be otherwise.

This subject came to my mind recently when I heard that one of the most exciting events that I can remember from my boyhood was going to be revived in Alameda, California. When I attended grammar school in Alameda, the highlight of the year was the cross-city relay. The competitors were the four grammar schools — Porter (which I attended), Haight, Lincoln, and Washington.

The race started at the west end of town and ended several miles away in Lincoln Park in the east end. All the youngsters who were not in the race sat in the colorfully bedecked stands, each school separate, anxiously watching the entrance to the park to see which school's runner would be first to come through the gate.

Each relay team consisted of 66 boys. They ranged from the 70-pounders to the heaviest. The 70-pounders from each school started the race, and the larger boys finished. We trained for this great event for many weeks. Much of the training consisted of practicing passing the baton, or "stick" as we liked to call it.

Every boy who ever participated in this race had a secret dread which never left him until the race was over. The dread was that he might drop the stick, because if he did, the chance of his school's winning was almost certainly lost.

If given the choice on the morning of the race of dropping the stick or dying on the guillotine, I'm sure 90 percent of us would have chosen the latter. It happened to one poor soul, and he never lived it down. Years later he was still referred to as "the boy who dropped the stick." On the day of the race I was, as were many others, physically sick from nervousness. Just writing about it causes me to relive those feelings.

For the last few years Porter had been finishing far behind. Then we had a new vice-principal, a Mr. Titus, who served as coach. He introduced us to a revolutionary new way of passing the baton.

In the past, we had stood sideways as the runner with the stick approached. Then we began trotting slowly, still watching him, until the stick was safely in our hand. Only then would we start running full speed.

Mr. Titus changed all this. We were now to place our entire trust in each other. As soon as the boy with the stick came within a certain distance, we were to turn our backs on him completely, stretch out our arm behind us, and start running at full speed. The runner would slap the stick in our outstretched hands — hopefully — and very little ground would be lost in the passing.

This particular year Porter was given no chance to win because our runners were no faster than they had been in previous years. Imagine the bedlam that broke loose in the Porter section of the stands when the first runner to enter Lincoln Park wore the blue and white of Porter School. We won the race handily.

All of us on the winning team learned something that day. We learned that each of us was interdependent upon the other, and that each of us played an equal part.

The slowest runners in the race played as important a part as the fastest. Their responsibility to their team was just as great. Conversely, if the fastest runners had dropped the stick, the result would have been just as devastating as if it had happened to the slowest.

It is difficult to describe the feeling of pride we all felt upon returning to school the next day. It seemed as if the entire student body was one person. There were no "big shots" or heroes. We had all worked equally hard in perfecting this new method of passing the baton, and it was much more risky than the method used by the other schools. We knew it was this team dedication which enabled us to win.

As John Donne wrote, "No man is an island, entire of itself."

24

Happiness Is Not Dependent Upon Outside Conditions

If the letters I receive are any criterion, almost all of us have at least one aspect of our lives we would like to see changed.

Those I hear from firmly believe that their happiness is contingent upon this change taking place. As they cannot imagine any improvement in the future, this leads to a feeling of depression.

People write to me saying they have been miserable on their jobs for years but can't make the decision to try something else. Others are unhappily married. Some believe their health is failing and will continue to fail as they age.

Although the reasons for their frustration and unhappiness are many and varied, they have one thing in common: They have accepted the fact that nothing can be done to change the particular area of their life which is unpleasant, so they believe they are destined to remain unhappy.

This, of course, is approaching the problem area of one's life from the wrong direction. If you believe your

74

happiness is dependent upon existing circumstances, you will never be really happy.

When you affirm, "I would be happy if this situation did not exist," or, "If this circumstance would change I would get along fine," you are impressing your subconscious mind with the belief that happiness is impossible for you unless certain conditions are met.

Coming to the realization that it is possible to be happy and contented even though existing circumstances are unfavorable requires a drastic change in one's thinking. The first thing that must be done is to do away with your conception of time, as you now know it.

If you are like most people, you have always looked to the future for the changes that would bring you happiness. Now you must develop a new concept. You must endeavor to train yourself to believe that the objects of your desires are already in existence and available to you, even though intellectually you know they are not.

It might be helpful to know that many great teachers throughout history have taught the methods to accomplish this. The Greek philosopher Plato and the Swedish author and philosopher Swedenborg, although separated by centuries — as well as many Eastern philosophers — suggested that we are to imagine there is a spiritual prototype of every existing thing in the universe.

Everything in the material world, they taught, is only an outgrowth of this spiritual prototype. (A physical prototype is an actual model after which anything is formed. A spiritual prototype, although it cannot be seen, is just as real.)

If you consistently imagine that the unseen prototype exists for you as if it were a physical one, it will eventually materialize regardless of apparent conditions.

75

This philosophy coincides with that given in the Bible in Mark 11:24. In this passage we are told that we can have anything we desire if we have enough faith to believe it already exists for us.

Eliminate from your mind all thoughts that your happiness is dependent upon a change in your job, your marriage, or anything else. See yourself as being happy in the same circumstances which are now causing you to be unhappy. Act happy even though you are not!

It won't be long before conditions will be forced to correspond to this change in your attitude. You will attract new circumstances which will supercede the unsatisfactory ones.

You will never eradicate an unhappy situation by giving it power to upset you. If you learn to accept happiness in the present, despite an undesirable situation, the situation will change to correspond to the change in you.

External conditions must eventually correspond to your thoughts. Whatever you think about with emotion will attract the conditions necessary to cause your thought to materialize.

25

Overcoming Habits Depends Upon Inner Change

It is unlikely that significant changes will occur in your life until you yourself change. You might resolve, with all the good intentions in the world, to attain certain goals or give up undesirable habits, but almost inevitably your resolve will fail.

The attaining of your goal must become more desirable to you than whatever has been keeping you from attaining it; the habit you are trying so hard to give up must lose its appeal. Until this happens your efforts — however good your intentions or great your resolve — will probably be in vain.

The compulsive gambler, the heavy drinker, and the obese are often motivated by fear or the admonition of others to reduce or stop that which is harmful to their well-being. Unless an inner change has happened, however, their efforts will be short-lived.

When you discontinue something you have been doing regularly, you automatically create a vacuum in your life. It is said that nature abhors a vacuum. If you do not take deliberate steps to fill it with something different, it will soon be refilled with that which you gave up.

As an example, poker parlors are available for those who enjoy plaing cards for money. This is a relatively harmless pastime and affords them many hours of pleasure. For others, however, it is an insidious disease which often leads to the loss of their homes and the breakup of families. For those unfortunates, will power alone will never keep them from returning to the tables.

Drinking falls into the same category. It is a pleasant pastime for some and a killer for others. Those who eat and drink too much are seldom able to generate enough will power to make a sustained effort to stop or cut down their intake.

It is always better to go along with nature than to go against it. We know a vacuum will be created when a habit is deleted from our life, and nature will always take steps to see that the vacuum is filled. We should, therefore, make sure the vacuum will be filled with something of our choice, rather than the same habit we are striving so desperately to overcome.

When steps are taken in advance to ensure that we make the right choice, two things happen, both of which are advantageous.

First, we become better prepared to withstand the shock of giving up something that has become addictive. The shock is not nearly so great when there is something to replace it.

The second is perhaps even more important, although it is intangible. In the process of developing other interests to replace the unwanted habit or habits, a gradual change of consciousness takes place in the individual, possibly unknowingly.

The person's attention becomes focused elsewhere, and it is this transferring of attention which makes the difference. Rather than concentrating upon not gambling, not drinking, or not overeating, one should direct his energy and attention to the replacement.

Gradually, the new thing will become more appealing than that which was given up. This factor accounts for the apparent miraculous change in character I have witnessed in so many habitual criminals. The change that took place in their lives was not caused by a sudden influx of will power, although a certain amount is necessary, especially in the beginning.

The most important factor, in my opinion, was the development of a new interest, which gradually became more important to them than their former way of life. Thus the former convict Don lost interest in frequenting bars and pushing drugs because of his newfound interest in graphology, which he is still pursuing with great success.

Others became so fascinated and excited with the changes for the better in their lives as a result of focusing their minds in new directions that they directed their efforts toward helping others do the same.

The development of new interests creates an inward change which makes the breaking of habits less painful.

26

Base Decisions on Fact, Not Theory

During my years as a salesman I have had the opportunity to make many interesting observations. For example, I have observed that top executives and owners of businesses are as susceptible to preconceived ideas and preconceived objections as anyone. Unfortunately, they do not always investigate to learn if these ideas and objections are correct.

Many make the same mistake in their personal lives. They follow patterns of living without stopping to ask themselves if it is the best way. If they did, they might discover that the reason they are doing as they are is that they are following the patterns of others instead of basing their decisions on their own intelligence and intuition.

Executives and owners who base their decisions on the opinions of others without personal thought and investigation cause many business failures. It is admittedly difficult for an executive to change a policy or to change his own belief concerning an issue. It may be tantamount to conceding that his former policies and ideas were erroneous.

A far greater mistake, however, is to refuse to consider the possibility that he might have been wrong, and that an improvement in the situation is still possible.

Sometimes it is almost inconceivable to observe the false thinking and beliefs many top executives hold on the same subject. It is as if one says, "This is obviously the reason for the problem," so the others accept his statement without question. All future decisions are then based on the supposition that the reason given was correct. But what if it is wrong?

Here is a classic example. I will present it briefly because readers in other parts of the country may not be as familiar with the subject as we in California.

For the past several years the San Francisco Giants baseball team has suffered from poor attendance, despite the fact that baseball has been enjoying great popularity elsewhere. This was generally considered by those in command to be due to the fact that for the past nine or ten years the Bay Area had two big league teams, Oakland being the other. Prior to the arrival of the Oakland team, the Giants had the area to themselves.

As everyone accepted this as the reason for the poor drawing power of both teams, steps were taken to transfer one to another city, although this has not materialized.

In coming to this decision, two factors were apparently overlooked. One was that for the past few years the Giants have had lack-lustre, losing teams and unimaginative ownership, which would cause poor attendance figures anywhere.

For the past two years they have had new owners who are progressive and promotion-minded, and this year the team is currently in first place. As a result, by the first of July their attendance far surpassed the total for the entire year of 1977.

Oakland's attendance has also improved, even though rumors of the team's transfer to another city have been prevalent since before the season's start. They also have a winning team.

The other factor that was overlooked by those who make the decisions was this: In the mid-forties, long before big league baseball came to the West Coast and when the population was much less, both Oakland and San Francisco drew exceedingly well with minor league teams. Furthermore, in the depression years of the thirties, San Francisco fielded two teams and Oakland one, and all three survived for years.

The point is that businesses, as well as individual lives, can be ruined because of assumptions that may be entirely false.

The child who is told he or she is "too dumb" to ever amount to anything will believe it, and a whole life will be adversely affected. The firm whose management accepts as gospel truth the negative ideas and thoughts of the gloom spreader is bound to suffer.

Every policy and decision will automatically be based on the premise that business in the future will be bad. Unfortunately, with this kind of attitude these assumptions will prove to be correct.

The real tragedy is that many have been conditioned to think like robots, instead of going within to look for the true answers. We should all ask ourselves, "Is this what I really believe or am I just going along with the mass thought on the matter?"

Victor Frankle, the great Vienese philosopher, said this when asked to define the difference between humans and animals: "Animals are driven, humans make decisions."

27

When Marriage Partners Change

Some blame the breakup of their marriage on the changes that have taken place in the spouse throughout the years. The fact is, in many cases, the spouse is essentially the same as he or she was in the beginning of the marriage.

It is the other who has changed, so that the qualities that were once endearing and amusing are now boring and perhaps even distasteful.

We are inclined to judge one not so much by what he does or how he acts but the way we feel about the person at the time he is acting in that particular way.

I was reminded of this fact once again when I met a woman I hadn't seen for years, and she told me of the breakup of her marriage. I had last seen her at a meeting my wife and I attended in the early 1960's. She was then newly married; her husband, a professional man, was the master of ceremonies. He evidently considered himself a comedian, but his attempts at humor were almost pathetic.

As well as I can remember, there were only two people in the entire audience who agreed with his evaluation of himself. You no doubt have guessed the first, and the other was his wife. Each roared with laughter after every so-called joke. The fact that they were alone in their appreciation of his humor in no way discouraged either of them.

I remember wondering at the time whether her approval of what many would consider a negative quality in him would last. My doubts were well-founded. She was now telling me that wherever they went he tried to be "the life of the party," and it became so embarrassing and obnoxious to her that she was seeking a divorce.

Could this same type of situation be the reason for the disintegration of so many marriages? The same actions and "quaint" mannerisms that once endeared one to the other become a bore with the passing of time. The bored person, not willing to admit that it was only his reactions to the other that have changed, becomes disenchanted with the marriage itself.

An honest look back into the past would undoubtedly remind this person that these same mannerisms were either overlooked entirely or looked upon with approval in the beginning of their courtship.

The important point to consider is that in this case, as in most others, neither the wife's reaction to, nor judgment of, her husband was based on reality. This includes her original approval of his actions and her later disapproval.

The first image the newly married woman held of her husband was a result of her love for him. An image based upon love alone can be unrealistic. The second image, which changed with the passing of time, is equally unrealistic and is unfair to her husband. After all, it is she who has changed, not he.

The passing of judgment on another causes problems in a marriage or any other close relationship. It is not only unjust to the person who has remained the same, as the husband in this case, but it is also unfair to the one who has changed.

An example is the way people react to those who have spent time behind bars. "Once a thief, always a thief," they say. Therefore, they classify the ex-convict accordingly. This type of branding, which appears to be universal, almost automatically nullifies any chance for the former criminal to make a successful new start in life.

Many cannot accept the fact that a change in one's character is possible. As harmful as this may be to the person involved, it is infinitely worse for the one passing judgment. One need look no further than the Bible for proof of this: "Judge not lest ye be judged."

We do not always judge others according to what they do but rather on the basis of whether what they do is currently pleasing to us. This attitude, of course, is unfair. Understanding and communication are necessary if a marriage is to be held together after the "bloom" is off. The better alternative to judging the other is to take a long look at yourself first. Looking at yourself through your partner's eyes may serve to open your own.

Someone has said, "We do not judge others by what they are in themselves but by what they are relative to us."

28

Overcoming Jealousy

Some Eastern philosophies recognize that there are three types of people. There are the creators, the preservers, and the destroyers.

Every person has some of each of these tendencies in his nature, but usually one is predominant.

The word "destroyer" in this context does not necessarily mean one who wreaks havoc physically. The dictionary explains that "to destroy" is the exact opposite of "to preserve."

The one who is extremely jealous and possessive would be classified as a destroyer. There is probably no more certain way of destroying a marriage, or any close relationship, than this.

Jealousy can be compared to an insidious disease, but, as with all diseases, a cure is possible. Those who are unreasonably jealous invariably suffer from a lack of self-esteem, although this is not always apparent on the surface. This naturally leads to feelings of unworthiness. They don't believe they deserve the good that has come to them, so they live in constant fear of losing it.

Thus they become possessive to the degree that even a casual friendship or relationship of their mate is resented, or even time spent with the other's family. This, of course, serves to make the marriage intolerable.

Those who suffer the pangs of jealousy are constantly filled with feelings of anxiety and apprehension which make life miserable for themselves and the ones closest to them. They are unable to acknowledge that the marriage partner is an individual who needs to be respected as such.

One's understanding of the misery the jealous person is undergoing will tend to make the marriage or relationship more bearable. Permanent improvement, however, will not take place until the jealousy itself is overcome.

If this is to be accomplished, a change in the person's belief concerning himself or herself is the first prerequisite. What can the jealous person do?

Realize there is a great therapeutic value in the practices of praise and devotion. If you are jealous and possessive, you are more likely to condemn yourself than to praise. To overcome this fatalistic tendency, refuse to entertain any negative thoughts about yourself. This will take perseverance and time. You will need to stand guard at the doorway of your mind and deny all negative thoughts the right to enter.

It will help if you will concentrate upon the positive aspects of your life, rather than on the negative. Everyone fails occasionally, and so do you. On the other hand, what about your accomplishments? Stop blaming yourself for your failures and give yourself credit where credit is due.

Your life is a reflection of your beliefs about yourself. As you hold onto certain beliefs, everything you do will serve to reinforce them. Therefore, if you retain feelings of inadequacy concerning yourself, your actions will serve to prove that your feelings were correct.

You inwardly expect to lose your loved one, so you will act accordingly. Your subsequent actions, based on your jealous nature, will alienate the one person you love above all others, and your unconscious beliefs will be fulfilled.

Many persons experience difficulty in improving their self-image for the same reason others find it difficult to experience happiness. It is not for lack of trying, but their energies are focused in the wrong direction. They are constantly looking for changes to take place in their outside circui1 tances rather than seeking to initiate a change in theil.selves.

Many of the negative concepts you now hold of yourself are based upon opinions that others drilled into you when you were very young. They are probably false, so begin the process of discarding them one by one. Write them down and then proceed to cross them off, signifying your refusal to accept them any longer. Focus your attention on your own positive attributes.

As your self-esteem grows, your jealousy and your need to feel overly possessive will fade away of its own accord.

You will become a preserver and creator instead of a destroyer.

29

Don't Give Power to the Past

One's skills or aptitudes do not always remain the same but will change as the outer situation changes. For this reason, success and failure are not always predictable. The same person may excel under one set of circumstances but in another his performance might be classified as mediocre.

The change from excellence to mediocrity can occur in a matter of minutes or seconds, depending upon the situation. The champion, or the one who stands above all others, is not affected by changes but accepts them and adjusts accordingly.

Visualize a pitcher and a batter as they face each other in a baseball game. Several pitches may be thrown, but only one final pitch will determine the result of this particular time at bat. Regardless of whether the previous pitches were 'balls or strikes, this final pitch will result in a walk, a hit, a strikeout, or an out by some other means.

However, the previous pitches will play a large part in determining the final outcome for the pitcher and the batter. For example, if the count reaches three balls and no strikes, the batter becomes a better hitter and the pitcher's skill diminishes; the batter gains more confidence, and the pitcher loses some. Conversely, if the count were to reach two strikes and no balls, the opposite would be true. The participants remain the same, but they allow their performance to be affected by what has gone before.

We constantly face parallel situations in our daily lives, perhaps without being conscious of it. As do the pitcher and the batter, we allow our performances to be affected by past events, instead of facing each situation as it occurs.

If we would face life one day — or one moment — at a time, and each event as an isolated incident, we would become more productive and our lives more peaceful.

How many times have you faced the day with the feeling you already have two strikes against you? When you do, is it because you are allowing happenings of the preceding day or days to color your outlook on the present?

The tendency to allow this to happen is extremely difficult to overcome. I doubt that any but the exceptionally well-disciplined regard everything that happens to them as a separate incident, without permitting it to affect their attitude or response to present events.

The salesman who makes several consecutive unsuccessful presentations will surely allow them to affect the quality of his next presentation. How much more effective he would be if he regarded each call as being distinct from the others. His situation is similar to that of the batter with two strikes on him, and who becomes a less effective hitter.

When one experiences several unproductive days in a row, it becomes increasingly difficult to reverse the situation. This is true in almost any job.

The remedy lies in seeing each situation as separate from all others and then facing it as it is, not as it might have been. If you do this, no time or energy is wasted in bemoaning the fact that it happened or why it happened.

If you are realistic, you know you cannot change what has happened in the past. With that understanding, you can proceed to form your future by your subsequent actions.

Once something happens, accept it, then proceed to adjust to it and take steps to rectify it. Don't give it the power to remain a negative factor in your life.

What you do today will have a profound influence on what happens to you tomorrow. What you did yesterday has a great influence upon what happens to you today. The difference is that you can choose the way you will act today; what you did yesterday is already done. You are powerless to change yesterday except as you develop a different attitude toward it.

When you are at bat, the only pitch you need be concerned with is the next one. In life, only what you do from now on is important. The past is over and done with.

30

Act As If

Many people tell me they are frustrated because they do not believe they are living up to their potential.

They are in a situation or a position where they are unable to express themselves as much as they would like to do. This is blamed on their job, their marriage or sometimes on the community.

Because of this feeling of frustration, some move from one job or one marriage partner or one community to another, but the happiness and fulfillment they seek continues to elude them. These people seldom give their current situation much of a chance before moving onto another.

Many are dissatisfied with their job, for example, and so do not put much effort into it. Then they wonder why it gives them little satisfaction in return.

It is true that some jobs are routine and unchallenging, but there is one cardinal rule which it is always advantageous to follow. (This holds true for many facets of life.) If you wish for something better than you now have, first do the best you can with what you do have.

No matter how high your aspirations, you must start from where you are now. Few seem willing to face this irrefutable fact. This does not mean to infer that we should accept whatever situation we are in as unchangeable. It does mean that sometimes patience and perseverance will lead to greater rewards than constantly jumping from one situation to another.

Most people seem to have little or no conception of how powerful they really are. They are unable to accept the fact that a change for the better is not necessarily dependent upon outside conditions changing. If this were not true, few would ever effect a change for the better in their lives except by chance.

For instance, those who graduated from high school or college during the "Great Depression" of the 1930's had no choice of jobs whatever, because so few were available. If they were lucky enough to stumble upon a job, they usually stayed with it whether they liked it or not. Many were waiting in line to replace them if they left, and there was no unemployment insurance to sustain them. Those who married early and had families were especially reluctant to make a change, even though they may have been in jobs for which they were unsuited.

There were some, however, who refused to accept the fact that depressed economic conditions had the power to control their lives. They did look for and find other positions which brought forth their full potential.

An identical situation seems to be evolving today. Jobs that one had every reason to believe were secure are disappearing because of shifting political situations, as well as changing economic conditions. Also, there are many who have prepared themselves for careers that now offer fewer and fewer opportunities.

It is easy for those who have been thus affected to give in to the situation and accept their lot without question. If they take the attitude that conditions over which they believe they have no control will prevent them from realizing their goals they will continue to be frustrated.

If you are one of these, try the following experiment for one day at a time. Deliberately change your attitude about whatever is making you unhappy. If your job is boring and uninspiring to you, accept this in itself as a challenge. Decide that for one day you will give it 100 percent of your attention and ability. Act as if you find the work exciting.

This principle is effective in any situation, including your marriage. Greet your husband or wife tonight as if you have been very happy together, even though you may not have been. Put more into the relationship without expecting anything in return. Act the way you acted when you were very much in love, but do not demand equal treatment.

As you discover that it is within your power to improve any area of your life by taking control over your attitude concerning it, you will regain the confidence in the future you thought was lost forever.

A great writer and philosopher from the past named Zacharias said, "Man is the favorite of nature, not in the sense that nature has done everything for him, but that she has given him the power of doing everything for himself."

31

Develop a Vivid Imagination

It is nature's way always to go forward. Therefore, when one does little or nothing productive, it can be compared to swimming against the current. You don't get very far but you still expend a lot of energy. The successful person flows with life and is constantly progressing. The failure remains stagnant.

The failure overlooks the fact that those who are successful also failed many times in the process of becoming successful. The basic difference is that the successful person refuses to accept his failure as final. On the contrary, he accepts his success as being certain. He sets the wheels in motion and knows that so long as he perseveres it is only a matter of time until he reaches his goal.

His confidence is not based on conceit, or a false belief in his worth, but rather on his knowledge of natural laws. He has seen the final result in his mind and knows that once something is established on the mental plane, it must and will materialize.

This is one of the great differences between those who are happy, well-adjusted, and in charge of their lives and those who are not.

The successful person acts as if his success were a foregone conclusion and proceeds accordingly. The failure proceeds with misgivings, and memories of past failures dominate his mind.

For example, many persons feel compelled to try to eradicate an undesirable habit, even though they know deep down inside they are not sincere. They have no intention of following through with their resolve; it is simply an unconscious attempt to appease their conscience. There is no real desire to give up their indulgences; they are only seeking justification for continuing them.

They have tried, they assure themselves, so now they can proceed with their self-gratification free from self-condemnation.

A vivid imagination is helpful if one is to attain fulfillment. Those who are able to act the part of a successful person before they actually achieve success will not fail in anything they undertake.

It is extremely important to free yourself from all reactions that result from past experiences, as well as fear of the future. Don't believe that your success depends upon any one course of events or upon the actions of other people. If you have developed the faculties of your imagination, this will not be necessary.

You will be able to envision your objective as already reached, and all of your concentration will be on this, instead of how or when it will happen. You will find that you will be subconsciously led to the means of its fruition. Make sure the image you hold in your mind is of your own choosing. No one can or should do this for you.

A reader sent me a dissertation by a writer named W.H. Murray. I am happy to quote it because it coincides with what I have so often emphasized: There is a great spiritual force within each of us, but it will remain dormant until called upon. We must take the first step.

Here is what Murray wrote:

> Until one is committed there is hesitancy, the chance to draw back, always ineffectiveness. Concerning all acts of initiative (and creation) there is one elementary truth, the ignorance of which kills countless ideas and splendid plans: The moment one definitely commits oneself, then providence moves too.

> All sorts of things occur to help one that would never otherwise have occurred. A whole stream of events issues from the decision, raising in one's favor all manner of unforeseen incidents and meetings and material assistance, which no man could have dreamed would have come his way.

> I have learned a deep respect for one of Goethe's couplets:

> "Whatever you can do, or dream you can, begin it. Boldness has genius, power, and magic in it."

All the great teachings attest to this concept. Throughout the eastern philosophies, it is written that when the student takes the first step toward his guru, or higher self, his guru will take ten toward him.

Ralph Waldo Emerson said, "The world belongs to the energetic."

32

You Are in Control

When one is emotionally disturbed or angry, it is very difficult to control the mind. The longer the emotions remain out of control, the more the body is adversely affected. We are constantly being advised that the mind has a direct influence on the body and its functions.

The next time you feel your emotions are getting out of control, you might wish to try some "reverse psychology." Do not overlook the fact that the actions of the body exert an influence upon the mind and have as much effect upon the emotions as the emotions have upon the body.

Physical actions are sometimes easier to control than are the processes of the mind, and the end result or goal of relaxation and peace will be the same either way. In order to become calm and relaxed, we must realize that just as the nature of our thoughts causes us to behave in a certain way, so do our bodily actions react upon the mind and influence our mental states.

Most of us are aware that an upset state invariably results in physical actions such as clenching fists, frowning, or grinding teeth. Those who have permitted these mannerisms to become habitual are producing a highly charged emotional state within themselves simply by doing so.

Therefore, just as an emotional state will cause these actions to occur, so will the actions themselves cause an emotional state. If you observe the people who are short-tempered and quick to fly off the handle, you will notice they are subject to many nervous habits. For example, the person who is perpetually scowling and clenching his fists is creating a state of tension so that it takes very little to cause him to become angry and upset.

All of this information is inconsequential unless we apply it to making our daily lives more tolerable, if not happier and more peaceful. Therefore, try this experiment:

No matter how you feel as you read this, and no matter how you may dread the day ahead, force a slight smile to form on your lips and in your eyes. Maintain this pleasant expression as constantly as you can throughout this and every day until it becomes automatic.

You will find that, although the situations which formerly upset you may still occur, they will occur less frequently. You will also find that you will react quite differently to them.

The physical act of smiling has helped you to become calm and relaxed just as surely as your being calm and relaxed would have caused you to smile.

Most of us go through life waiting and hoping for happiness and peace of mind. This principle will help you attain them. Change your physical actions to conform to the way you would act if you were in a state of happiness and well-being now, even though you are not. You will then attract people and circumstances to correspond with your pleasant mood.

A late, well-known writer and teacher named Neville explained it better than I can. He said:

"If a physical state can produce a psychological state, a psychological state can produce a physical fact. If the effect (a) can be produced by the cause (b), then inversely, the effect (b) can be produced by the cause (a)."

Perhaps this is the reason the Bible constantly stresses the importance of faith — not ordinary faith, but the kind that enables one to believe in that which he has not yet seen.

Contrary to what we may have believed since childhood, we have the power within us literally to "turn things around" without waiting for outside circumstances to change first. Smiling even though you don't feel like smiling is a good beginning.

Everyone can use these principles to advantage. If you are unable to get rid of negative emotions such as fear, worry, and anger by controlling your mind, try controlling your body instead. Control of the mind will follow automatically.

Instead of letting circumstances determine how you will think and act, deliberately reverse the situation. Strive for a state of relaxation, and the negative emotions will disappear of their own accord.

33

Overcome Fear through Understanding

Two very traumatic happenings occur to many of us in early childhood.

The first occurs when we discover our parents are far from perfect. This experience shatters an illusion we had from the time it was natural for us to place them on a pedestal. When those whom we most respect "fall from grace," it leaves us with a feeling of uncertainly that may last throughout our lives.

The second disturbing period comes with the concept that God is up in the heavens watching our every move, ready to punish us for every wrongdoing. This thought causes one to be extremely fearful; to be fearful of God instead of loving Him.

It is the fearful attitude people have that concerns me. There can be no feeling of inner security for one who is in constant fear of being punished, especially when there are so many different versions of what is "right" and "wrong."

Many are ill at ease and frustrated because they have lost confidence in almost everything and everyone. They find it difficult to know in whom or in what to believe.

102

This feeling of fearfulness and mistrust affects the impression they maintain of themselves. If one is to have a sense of security, he must be able to believe in something beyond doubt. He must also believe in himself and in the fact that he is responsible for his own thoughts and actions.

More importantly, he must realize that his every thought and action must have a consequence — not that it *may* have but that it *must* have.

The idea that there is a vengeful God waiting to punish us, and that He has no compassion, is enough to cause severe mental anguish in anyone. I believe this idea to be false, although I respect the opinions of those who believe it to be true. I believe the desire to punish is a human weakness, not a godly attribute.

If there is one natural law in which you can believe with utmost confidence, it is the law of cause and effect. There definitely will be a consequence to every action! Instead of this knowledge causing a sensation of fear, however, it should cause a feeling of confidence in, and hope for, the future. If you actions are causing you unhappiness, change them, and the effect will change.

When your life is not going smoothly, instead of bemoaning the fact and blaming the problem on someone else, consider this analogy:

If your car is not running properly, something is out of harmony. Perhaps some wires are crossed or some parts need adjusting. Now, what happens when the adjustments are made? The car runs more smoothly. You don't think about punishing the car for not operating efficiently. You realize it was only a matter of putting all the parts back in harmony with each other.

It is the same with our lives. If we are fearful and suspicious or allow ourselves to harbor resentments, it will be virtually impossible to experience harmonious relationships with anyone over a period of time. Obviously, this lack of harmony cannot be blamed on God but only on ourselves.

It becomes apparent that we have been put here to learn and grow.

If you can begin with the premise that you control much of what happens to you, you will find it much easier to accept yourself as you are.

You will agree that certain adjustments in your character and personality are necessary if the desired improvements and changes are to take place. You will also become aware that these changes and improvements are within your power to make.

Take the attitude that you have some wonderful material with which to work and proceed at your own pace. We are constantly learning, so we are bound to make mistakes. This fact does not mean there is reason to be fearful. When we make mistakes, life becomes more difficult until we rectify our mistakes.

This is our punishment. It is also our reward.

34

You Can't Get Something for Nothing

It seems that every time you look at the paper or turn on the radio you read or hear of someone taking advantage of someone or of some situation.

This problem is not limited to individuals. Large corporations appear to have lost their integrity and are not concerned with the best interests of their customers. The adage, "honesty is the best policy," seems to have gone out of style.

These observations are not true, of course, of all individuals or all companies. But it is true that shady dealings or wrongdoing are no longer frowned upon to the extent that they once were.

Some people believe it is foolish to pass up an opportunity to make an extra buck, regardless of the means employed. Many of our youth are being instilled with the philosophy that they should look out for themselves first and not be concerned for the welfare of others.

I wonder whether those who believe this way and act accordingly realize they are taking a terrible gamble. I am referring not only to the chance they take of going to prison. This is obvious. When one takes the position that his actions will have absolutely no bearing on his future, he is refuting virtually everything that has been handed down to us throughout the centuries.

If nothing else, he is putting his self-esteem and peace of mind on the line. If that isn't a big gamble, what is?

It is relatively easy for a person to drift into the habit of being dishonest and taking advantage of others whenever the opportunity presents itself. One seldom sees the immediate penalties of even the most flagrant violations of the law. Of all the crimes committed, only about 19 percent result in arrests, and less than five percent of these result in convictions.

Seemingly, then, crime does pay. If being apprehended and convicted were the only considerations, it is understandable that some would be willing to take the chance. This is not the case, however. There is much more at stake!

Those who believe that their only concern should be for their own self-gratification evidently are absolutely certain that there is no "payment due" of any kind after their physical death. The chance of gaining material possessions by dishonest means does not justify the terrible loss one would experience if that which has long been taught by all the great religions and philosophies is true — that one must reap what he sows.

Those who think they can get something for nothing will have to learn the hard way that it is not true. In the long run, everyonè receives in direct proportion to what he gives. This is a natural law from which no one is exempt.

Nothing is free, even though it may take the passage of time to prove this. The following story makes this point better than I can:

There once was a great king who wished all the wisdom of the ages to be made available to his subjects. He called all his philosophers together and instructed them to travel as far as necessary to gather and compile this information. Several years passed before they presented the king with many huge volumes of wisdom.

He was pleased but realized it was too much for his subjects to absorb. He told his philosophers to go forth again and bring back a condensed version. This they did, but several volumes were still necessary to hold the information they had gathered.

The king realized he would have to do something drastic. He told them they must condense all the wisdom of the ages into one sentence. This task took them longer than all the work they had done previously, and this is the sentence upon which they agreed:

"There is no such thing as a free lunch."

35

Expectations

Those who are happy and successful usually expect to continue to receive the good things of life. The people who are unsuccessful and unhappy much of the time take the opposite viewpoint. They take the attitude that the worst is yet to come.

In each case, results will invariably bear out their expectations.

This does not happen by accident. The subconscious mind does not reason; it simply follows orders. These orders come from the conscious mind, and the nature of one's expectations is vitally important.

The person who anticipates more and more success and happiness is making an impression on his subconscious mind, which accepts these suggestions without question. It will immediately take steps to see that his expectations are fulfilled.

The more successful one is, the easier it is for him to be optimistic and to have faith in the future. He is seldom disappointed. But what about his opposite? How is the unhappy person who considers himself a failure going to develop faith in the future?

One's expectations have a great bearing on one's attainments. The old saying is usually proved true: "The rich get richer, and the poor get poorer." According to the letters I receive, there are many persons who have little or no faith in the future. Their lack of faith is justified, at least on the surface, as it is based upon past failures.

This attitude can and must be changed if an improvement in one's life is to take place. The first step to take is to prepare for good to come in your life as if you really expected it.

It is important that you show your faith in physical ways as well as mental. If you desire a new wardrobe, for example, you should buy something for a starter, even if it is only a necktie or a scarf. Do this with the attitude that this is only the beginning and that the rest will follow as a matter of course.

This attitude is an expression of faith and will make a positive impression upon your subconscious mind. Don't limit yourself, or wonder by what means your wishes will be fulfilled. Leave the channels open. Otherwise, you will find yourself looking for all the reasons it can't happen.

It is important in the beginning that you believe you are worthy of that for which you are striving. You may not realize it now, but there may be some unforeseen adjustments to be made after the desired results are attained.

If you have a poor opinion of yourself, you will have a difficult time making these adjustments. I have had several letters from people with this problem.

A woman from Minnesota wrote me that she had spent most of her life expecting the worst. More often than not, her expectations were met! Then she followed my advice, became more optimistic, and her life began to change for the better.

Unfortunately, however, she continued to maintain a poor self-image. As a result, the good fortune which followed caused her to have guilt feelings. She also held the belief that it was "too good to be true," and that it could not last.

There is another factor which enters the picture when conditions or circumstances change suddenly for the better. The person involved may discover that considering himself "unworthy" or "unlucky" had given him a sense of security, or become a "crutch" which he is reluctant to give up. After all, if you feel you are unworthy, you have an excuse for not trying.

The woman from Minnesota who was faced with this problem was able to overcome it through understanding. She realized she would have to learn to think better of herself before she could accept the good that came to her. She also knew that she would have to give up the "crutch" that her belief in her unworthiness afforded her.

Strange as it seems, it is not always easy to adjust to change, even when the change is for the better.

36

Bend with the Blows

It isn't the real calamities that cause most of the unhappiness in life. In fact, many people seem better able to cope with serious setbacks than with the minor irritations of everyday life.

Those who permit themselves to be at the mercy of petty annoyances will probably be unhappy or discontented much of the time. They will become too rigid in their thinking and unable to change as the situations demand.

One must learn to bend.

If you will observe tall trees during a windstorm, you will notice they sway rather than remain rigid. This is why they survive. If they refused to bend they would snap.

It becomes easier to adjust when we realize there can never be any one prescribed way to judge a situation or a person. Current circumstances are often the determining factor, and circumstances are constantly changing. The sooner we learn to sway or bend as the occasion demands, the better for our peace of mind.

What might be perfectly acceptable to us in one set of circumstances might be objectionable in another. Therefore, if we judge everything from only one viewpoint — ours — we are not being realistic.

This does not mean we should change our code of ethics for any reason. I am referring to the minor irritations that we are constantly called upon to deal with in our everyday living.

Recently my wife and I were heading for Reno from Eastern Nevada. It was during the week, so I hadn't thought it was necessary to call ahead for reservations. Unexpectedly, however, we found all the Reno accommodations were taken. We decided to go to Carson City, 30 miles away.

It was 7 p.m., and there appeared to be many vacancies. As a result, we were selective and turned down the first few motels we investigated. All of a sudden, "No Vacancy" signs began to appear, and I realized that Carson City was getting Reno's overflow. It would be only a matter of time until the same situation would prevail there.

We hurried back to our first motel, which previously had not appealed to us at all. Now we considered ourselves fortunate to get the last available room.

When we heard later that people were sleeping in their cars, our entire viewpoint changed. The same room we would have been dissatisfied with under normal conditions now actually seemed desirable.

Had our attitude remained rigid, we would have been very annoyed to accept a room we had considered decidedly inferior a short time before.

It is not as easy to adjust when the reason for the annoyance or inconvenience is not as apparent as it was in this case. Still, we must learn to adapt, regardless of whether or not we understand the cause.

Another mistake many of us frequently make is judging others based upon our own beliefs and viewpoints. We don't approve of what they are doing, but we don't stop to consider that there may be circumstances of which we are unaware causing their behavior.

A little reflection will show you how foolish it is to give people or situations the power to upset and disturb you. Keep in mind that if you can control your reactions, people or situations have no power over you. Once you absorb the fact that your reactions are a matter of your own choosing, you will find it much easier to adapt.

Don't allow outside circumstances to make life miserable for you. Set high standards and ideals. Expect the best of yourself and of others. However, under certain situations, when you have to accept less than the best, be willing to bend and adjust to whatever the current circumstances demand.

No one can really let you down. It is true that another person may not live up to your expectations, but who are you to judge? You may not be living up to another's expectations of you!

37

Success Depends on Attitude

I have frequently wondered why some people find it almost impossible to achieve the goals they set for themselves while others find it relatively easy.

Perhaps an answer may be found by observing those who are successful.

The nature of the goal itself apparently is not a factor. The same principle applies whether the person is attempting to give up habits which he considers harmful, better his present position, raise his income, or improve his physical condition through an exercise program.

When you see a person who is obviously successful and in excellent condition, you may wonder how he had the will power and self-discipline required to attain that state. Then you may wonder why others — and perhaps yourself — are unable to accomplish the same.

The difference is the attitude with which each approaches the situation. Almost without exception, those who habitually fail approach any form of self-improvement from a negative viewpoint. The first word that comes to their minds is "sacrifice."

The successful person takes the opposite approach.

The first word that comes to his mind is "opportunity." Instead of focusing his mind on those things he will be doing without, as does the failure, he will concentrate upon the opportunity to better himself.

We should avoid the use of words which imply that a rigid program of self-discipline and denial will be necessary. As an example, those who wish to lose weight should never use the word "diet." Instead of "I am going on a diet," it would be far better to say, "I am going to change my eating habits so that I will look and feel better!"

Your success or failure in any undertaking will depend to a great extent on your mental attitude at the start. Therefore, before determining what physical actions must be taken for the fulfillment of your goals, work on your mental attitude. If this remains the same as when you failed in the past, your chances for success are minimal.

It stands to reason that if you are to be consistent with any program, you must enjoy what you are doing. The men I see regularly at the health club to which I belong obviously enjoy doing their exercises. Most of those who join thinking they will go through a period of rigid self-discipline soon drop out.

Somewhere along the line — usually in the very beginning — the successful person determined in his own mind where his priorities should lie. He reached the conclusion that the attainment of his goals was infinitely more important than that which he would be required to give up in order to attain them.

When he reached this point, much of the feeling of self-sacrifice and self-denial was automatically eliminated, as was the need for an excessive amount of will power. After all, it doesn't require will power to give up something when you know you will gain in the long run.

Those who are progressing toward the realization of a goal have forgotten, for the most part, those things they were required to deny themselves along the way. This fact does not necessarily mean they are stronger than the rest of us. The difference is that they have learned to place their attention on the achievement of the goal, rather than upon the obstacles that stand in the way.

I know this to be true from my own experience. For many years I was a heavy smoker and, although I vowed many times to quit, I was always unsuccessful except for short periods. I was unable to conceive of myself going through certain situations without a cigarette.

Finally, I set a date about three weeks ahead when I would "stop for good." However, this time there was a difference from my numerous other unsuccessful attempts.

During the entire period, I forced myself to think only of the positive aspects of not smoking — of which there are many! By the time the appointed day arrived I was actually in a state of anticipation. Instead of dreading the date I had set for giving up the habit, I looked forward to it as the beginning of a new life — which it turned out to be.

Much of the pain of stopping was eliminated. It wasn't a matter of suddenly developing more will power; it was simply a matter of changing my own mental attitude.

38

Some Questions and Answers

Over the years, I have received numerous questions in the mail and have tried to answer as many as possible personally. The answers I gave may not have been the correct ones but they were based on my own understanding of basic laws and principles.

In many cases, however, I received later reports that results obtained from following the simple principles bordered on the fantastic. Some of the questions and answers may be of interest:

Question: There appears to me to be a tremendous difference between the successful person and the failure. What is your opinion?

Answer: In my opinion, the difference is not very great or one that cannot be overcome. From my observations, the failure is constantly looking for and waiting for outside circumstances to change. He believes that he is virtually helpless to improve conditions in his life on his own. As a consequence, this person may go through an entire lifetime "waiting for his ship to come in."

On the other hand, the successful person recognized early that before an outer change in his circum-

117

stances could take place, a change must take place in himself.

There is a thin line between a failure and a success, but the line still must be crossed. When you change inwardly, your outer circumstances must change to conform to your new inner beliefs. Success will follow as a natural result.

Question: I seem to have lost interest in life. What can I do?

Answer: Change your attitude. Stop worrying about not getting enough out of life and start becoming concerned about what you can put into it. When one loses interest in what is happening around him, he becomes overly concerned with his own problems. At this point life becomes dull because he himself is dull.

One way to make life more interesting is to become more interesting yourself. The first step is to get involved in anything that will take your mind off yourself and your problems. Go back in your life as far as is necessary until you discover something you once liked to do and then determine to pursue it. You will meet new people, and your life will take on new dimensions.

(The woman who asked this question remembered that as a child she had an aptitude for drawing and painting. She took some lessons and became extremely successful. Another derived great enjoyment from playing the piano, although she had not played for more than 50 years.)

Question: I have failed in everything I have ever undertaken. How can I reverse this?

Answer: You never really failed; you just gave up too soon. You stopped before the issue was decided. Edison tried 2,000 times before he found the final solution to the electric light. He did not consider his attempts failures, however; only 2,000 ways that did not work.

Most failures are caused by fear and lack of perseverance. When you start out, think of your success as being a foregone conclusion. Why consider failure at all?

Question: How can I overcome my regrets about the past?

Answer: This seems to be a universal problem. Someone once made the observation that all the mental hospitals in the country would be only half full the moment the inmates freed themselves from feelings of guilt. No one, of course, should ever feel he can do as he pleases, regardless of who is hurt.

However, carrying guilt feelings with you for the rest of your life won't help or solve anything. What is done is done, but resolve not to repeat the act.

From a religious standpoint, the Bible says we are punished not for our wrongs, but for our persistence in doing wrong. Whatever you did was probably the best you knew at the time. You may think now you knew better, but if you did, you would have done differently. The important thing is to do differently in the future. Then, if you continue to condemn yourself, you are condemning a person who no longer exists.

Be sure to make restitution where possible. If it is too late, because of death, treat someone else the way you wish you had treated the person who died.

39

More Questions and Answers

The answers to these questions are based upon my interpretation of principles which have long been taught, and not upon some theory that I thought up or claimed to discover. My reward comes from the letters I receive testifying that following these principles actually did improve these people's lives.

Question: I have been divorced for several years. My life is becoming increasingly dull, and I am afraid I am sinking into a state of depression. Although I am in reasonably good health and less than middle age, I feel the best part of my life is over. What can I do?

Answer: What seems a tragedy at the time may turn out to be a blessing, as unlikely as it may appear now. Many divorces, as traumatic as they are to all those involved, have proved to have been a new beginning.

I've personally known some who were terribly discouraged and would have remained that way if they had not made a determined effort to change their attitude toward their situation.

If we are somehow able to review our lives at the time of death, as some say we are, we would find many instances where a seemingly tragic experience turned out for the best in the long run. If the disheartened person would regard the unhappy event as a challenge and endeavor to look toward the future with confident expectation, he could quickly turn things around for himself.

The first step is to take your mind off your problems and take definite steps to improve yourself, both physically and mentally. This advice applies to anyone who is discouraged.

Make the Law of Attraction work for you. The way you look and the way you feel about yourself will determine the new people and new situations you will attract. Remember, today is the first day of the rest of your life.

You will be amazed at the wonderful changes that will take place the moment your attitude changes. You must accept the fact that the power to change things for the better lies within you and is not dependent upon others.

Question: Many of my peers and some of my best friends are drinking and/or are on drugs. What harm would there be in my joining them?

Answer: As we go through life, we are all constantly being faced with the necessity of making decisions. This is sometimes difficult, but this decision-making becomes easier when one faces up to this indisputable fact: Every act must have an aftermath — not *might* have but *must* have. It is true that we have freedom of choice, but it is also true that each act will have definite consequences.

We can take the words of two great thinkers who lived about 2,500 years apart as evidence for this:

Buddha said, "You can no more separate the action from its results than you can separate the sound of the drum from the drum."

121

Ralph Waldo Emerson said, "There is no dividing line between the act and the consequence of the act."

Knowing that every action must have a natural consequence, Emerson considered them as being one and the same.

I'll always remember the advice for young people given by an ex-convict named Don. He had formerly been a drug pusher and delighted in being tagged as a real tough character. A great change took place in him when he finally realized his peers, those he was trying so hard to impress, were nothing but a bunch of "losers" like himself.

Why play "follow the loser"?

Question: I have an easy job, plenty of leisure time, enough money, and yet I am discontented. Why?

Answer: You are not living up to your potential or probably even close to it. The more leisure time we have, the less contented many of us become. The one who spends the weekends watching football games on television is not as contented Sunday night as the one who spends them productively.

Put more into your job, and do more than you are expected to do. The closer you come to your potential, the more contented you will become.

40

All Things are Possible

The following strange series of events began in April or May, 1965, and culminated on a day in early October of last year.

I was conducting my first class at Folsom State Prison. There were about 50 men present, some who had come for the sole purpose of heckling and testing me. The class was scheduled to last three hours, and I was beginning to wonder how I would get through it. There were no guards present at the meeting.

I was also aware that if I failed this time there would not be another chance. In my meeting with the warden he had made it clear that in his opinion I was wasting my time trying to help the men, as they had no interest in anything. They certainly had no desire to better themselves.

Just when it seemed that the meeting was getting out of hand, one of the convicts rose from his seat, walked to the front of the room, and faced the group. When he spoke, everyone listened.

I found out later that, although he weighed only about 180 pounds, he was one of the strongest men in the world, having lifted 715 pounds. This fact was well-known by the others, and I was grateful for that.

I can remember Bill's words as if they were spoken yesterday, because they probably shaped both his future and mine.

"If you guys don't shut up you'll have to deal with me later," he snarled at them. "I understand this man is driving over 200 miles to try and help us in any way he can. I also know he receives no pay or expense money. If you can't show him some respect, get the hell out now and stay out!"

After that there wasn't a sound. Those who came to heckle may not have wanted to listen to me, but they sure didn't want to tangle with Bill. Thanks to this man's timely intervention, the meeting was a success, and from that day on I never experienced further heckling.

During the ensuing years, Bill never missed a meeting. He became a very positive influence in the prison and was personally responsible for helping many of the other convicts with his positive attitude and friendliness.

In 1974, my life began to take a new direction. I was invited to lecture to various groups in Contra Costa County (California) and later in other states. During one of my prison meetings, I said to Bill, "Someday you and I will lecture together. You will become as large an influence for good in the outside world as you now are in prison."

"Doug," he said, "that sure sounds great, and I'd like nothing better. However, you are forgetting one important fact: I'm serving a life sentence, and it looks like I'll never see the outside world again. I've already been confined for 16 years."

I told Bill that we should put into practice the teach-

124

ings we had learned and discussed during the years we had known each other.

"We will visualize ourselves speaking together on a program somewhere in the outside world," I said. "Never mind how it will happen. That does not have to be our concern. We will make a very strong mental picture of this, no matter how unlikely it seems now. I want you to start preparing for it and act as if the result is a foregone conclusion."

Bill immediately did what is always necessary if these laws and principles are to work for us. He didn't wait for something to happen; he took the first step. He became active in the Gavel Club, which is an offshoot of Toastmasters International, and eventually became an accomplished speaker.

Despite many reversals, he never faltered in his resolve to become a better person and set a good example for persons around him. It finally paid off for him, and after 18 years in Folsom Prison, Bill was released. He now has a good job and is highly regarded by everyone with whom he comes in contact.

Last October, the mental picture we had impressed upon our minds became a reality. I was invited to speak at Lost Medanos College in Pittsburg, California, and Bill shared the program with me.

I know there are many who believe they are victims of fate and are therefore powerless to change the circumstances of their lives. It is Bill's ambition to tell these people that there is always hope. He is a living example of the truth of the biblical saying, "All things are possible to him who believes."

125

41

Self Discipline Leads to True Freedom

In my opinion, the dictionary fails to give the true meaning of some words. The word "discipline" is one that comes to mind.

The definition leads us to believe that discipline is a form of chastisement or punishment. The dictionary gives the impression that the one who is disciplined by others, or even by himself, has somehow given up his freedom.

I would almost go so far as to say that the opposite is true. I have never seen anyone who demonstrates freedom as much as the one who has learned to discipline himself. Because he has not always done what he wanted to do when he wanted to do it, he is free to do as he likes.

Those who overindulge will suffer because of their indulgences or eventually be forced to give up completely what they formerly enjoyed. The alcoholic, the drug addict, and those who suffer from ill health because of heavy smoking or overeating are no longer free to enjoy liquor, drugs, smoking, or eating.

Freedom to enjoy these things was lost to them forever because of unwillingness to practice a certain amount of self-denial while there was still time. Now they are forced to deny themselves, whether they want to or not: Either do that or suffer what may be extreme consequences.

The person who refuses to practice any form of self-discipline makes a sorry picture as the years go by.

I'm not writing from a moral standpoint. Leave the moral issue out entirely, if you wish. It is more a matter of the individual doing what is best for himself in the long run.

To give you a different viewpoint, I might say it is a question of what will truly give the person the most pleasure. Heretofore, you probably assumed there is no pleasure when discipline is involved, but usually the opposite is true. A far better definition of the word "discipline" would be "control." This is much more appropriate than the words "punishment" or "chastisement."

Look around you and observe those who are obviously in control of themselves and their activities. Compare them with those who are not. Who are the happier? It is the undisciplined rather than the disciplined who are being punished!

The constant search for pleasure is bound to end in frustration. Each time a new pleasure is discovered, its appeal is soon lost, and so the search for something else must go on. After a time, the searcher becomes jaded. When this happens, virtually nothing is exciting.

An example is the person who drinks to excess. He must drink a certain amount in order to feel as good as he would if he didn't drink at all! When he stops, the inevitable letdown follows, so he must continue.

The process becomes a vicious cycle from which many persons never emerge. At this point, his only recourse is complete abstinence. Thus, through lack of discipline, he has forever deprived himself of his freedom to drink.

The question of discipline is pertinent in determining the degree of one's success or failure.

If you analyze the failure, you will find that he chooses the easiest method of doing a job. His main purpose is getting it done with the least possible effort. The successful person is concerned with good results and is willing to do whatever is necessary to achieve them.

A very successful person once said, "Success is something achieved by the minority of people, and it is therefore unnatural and not to be achieved by following our natural likes and dislikes, nor by being guided by our natural preferences and prejudices." He went on to say that successful people do the things that failures don't like to do.

Stop thinking of discipline as punishment. In some instances, it is best defined as love, as that given by a parent to a child. If you are a child and feel you are being subjected to too much discipline, keep in mind it would be much easier for your parents not to bother. At least you know someone cares about you.

42

Recognize the Need to Contribute

The word "responsibility" can be placed in the same category as the word "discipline." Nobody seems to want to have much to do with either, but it is impossible to get very far without them.

I made a discovery recently, mostly by accident, that may have a great deal of significance.

I was going over in my mind people I have known who were unable to cope. I have come in contact with many of these because of my prison work and also because of the nature of my writing. I constantly hear from and meet people with this type of problem. These are people who believe life isn't worth living so their existence is virtually meaningless.

I then tried to recall all those I knew who had "snapped out of it" or had made what I like to call a "comeback."

There were quite a number of them, and in every case one fact stood out. Each one, without exception, began to take on a degree of responsibility for his or her life, and as a result began to contribute.

The key word is "contribute." Those who find it hard to cope are probably contributing very little. Until they do, they will remain in their present state of inertia.

Those who have no sense of responsibility seem to believe that it is someone's duty to contribute to them. So long as they feel this way, nothing of any consequence is likely to happen.

I doubt if there is a better or quicker way to overcome depression or to change your life for the better than to begin to contribute in some way. There will be no long waiting period. The moment you start giving of yourself things will begin to happen. Don't let ignorance about how to get started be an excuse.

Some people I've known have emerged from their depression by looking for others who have the same problem. They then try to lead the way be setting an example.

I've witnessed this first hand many times in prisons. One man finds a new interest, such as joining the Gavel Club or taking a course, and his newfound enthusiasm encourages others to follow in his footsteps.

I used to think some situations were hopeless, but no more. I have seen many so-called hopeless cases turn out well.

One of the most dramatic was this: A convict, whom I'll call Arthur, had been placed in a "strip cell." A strip cell contains nothing at all except a hole in the floor. Once a day he was served bread and water. He had no friends, either in the prison or in the outside world. He had the reputation among the authorities of being absolutely incorrigible, and his sentence read "life without possibility of parole."

To use his own words, he said at this point he "had even less than when he started his own evolutionary process millions of years ago."

Not long ago we had him and his lovely wife to dinner at our house. He was bubbling over with enthusiasm, with plans to help other ex-convicts readjust to life on the outside.

He explained that the turning point in his life came when he realized that he and he alone was responsible for his life. He knew that if a change for the better were ever to take place it must take place within himself first!

As his attitude improved he was given more freedom within the prison. He began to look for ways to contribute. He attempted to give as many of the other convicts as he could the feeling of responsibility to contribute.

It is no accident when an immediate improvement in one's circumstances takes place. An improvement must take place because now the person's attention is no longer focused upon the negative aspects of his or her life, but on the welfare of others.

43

Mental Attitude Reverses Aging Process

Our society places too much importance upon a person's chronological age.

For example, it is difficult to obtain employment until you are a certain age; however, once you reach the so-called middle years, employment is equally hard to find. Then when you are 65, you are considered to be "over the hill" and so are retired.

A marriage is generally frowned upon if there is a wide divergence in years between the man and woman, even though they might be compatible in every way. The media constantly refers to an athlete as an "old-timer" if he is older than 30.

These concepts are apparently based upon the assumption that in some mysterious way, as we reach a certain age, physical and mental changes must occur automatically. Also, it is often implied that we are all exactly the same and that the passing of years has the identical effect on everyone.

Although a little reflection will make it obvious that these concepts and beliefs are false, they are nevertheless

132

dangerous. Too many people have gradually become conditioned to accept them without question. This situation results in many wasted years and lives virtually ending as the older person's productivity is halted much too soon.

It is tragic to hear someone say those unhappiest of words, "It's too late." I have heard this statement from some who are relatively young, as well as from the more mature.

A young man once said to me, "I've always wanted to be a dentist but never quite got around to taking the necessary steps. If I started now I would be 35 before I could begin my practice."

I said, "You will be 35 whether you are practicing dentistry or not. Hanging on to false beliefs concerning your age and your capabilities will prevent you from making the attempt. In that case, the result is a foregone conclusion."

The truth is that the body will, of course, eventually show the effects of age. However, how much of this deterioration is the result of our belief that it must happen?

One's expectations and the beliefs he holds concerning himself have a profound effect upon his life. Therefore, the body of one who is constantly looking for signs of its deterioration will in fact deteriorate more quickly than that of one whose mind is focused on the more positive aspects of life. Whatever you give your attention to becomes your experience.

It is not necessarily the number of years a person has lived that makes one old. One's mental attitude is more important, and this can be changed. You can change the way you think and believe, even though you cannot change the number of years you have lived.

133

As proof of this statement, there are people of all ages, young and old alike, who find it difficult to arise in the morning and they act as if they are in a daze most of the day. These are symptoms of old age, regardless of how many years have passed.

Being young means being excited about life, curious to learn and explore, confident you can handle whatever happens. Being old is being depressed, with no pleasurable anticipation for the future, a feeling that life is no longer worth living.

Chronological age has little to do with these two opposite viewpoints about life. There are many young people who fit into the second category, and just as many elderly who fit into the first. Both young and old should rid themselves of the false belief that their life is unalterable.

Old age is also having a feeling of anxiety, doubt, and fear. Often it is being cynical and ridden with guilt about the past. These negative emotions may afflict anyone. The number of years that have passed is not a factor.

Decide now to free yourself from all of the myths concerning aging to which you have been subjected.

Look for new interests. Even if bedridden or house-bound, you can become interested in new reading material. If your vision is impaired, listen to tapes, or develop a taste for beautiful music.

Get your mind away from your problems and look forward to a future that you have the power to create. As your life expands, you will be amazed how soon you begin to feel and look younger.

You are as young as your faith, as old as your doubts, as young as your hope, as old as your despair.

44

In Everything Give Thanks

Over the years I have gained a different perspective concerning Thanksgiving Day and the true meaning of giving thanks. This has helped to explain a Bible passage I have often quoted but had never been able to understand — "In everything give thanks" (Thessalonians 5:18).

In our large family, Thanksgiving Day had always been filled with excitement. My mother and father always made it a festive occasion, no matter how strained the financial circumstances at the time.

Each year I would write down all that I felt I should be thankful for. Some years, I must admit, the list was quite small, although I would try my hardest to stretch a point wherever possible.

I continued this practice into adulthood. One year, for some forgotten reason, I decided to list the "things to be thankful for" on one side of the paper and the "things not to be thankful for" on the other.

A few years ago I came across this list, which I had written so long ago. I was amazed at what I saw.

The happenings and events of the intervening years made me want to revise the list almost completely. In many instances, as things turned out, I should have given thanks for that which was listed on the "not thankful for" side, and the opposite was also true.

That experience completely changed my thinking and attitude concerning the day-to-day happenings of my life. It has helped me to withhold judgment as to whether what happens to me is "good" or "bad."

I have learned that given the perspecitve of time many episodes and events that we deem unfortunate are in reality for our best interests in the long run.

It is astonishing how much change in one's life a slight change of attitude such as this can make. It automatically eliminates many of the emotional highs and lows to which most of us are subjected.

There is an ancient Chinese tale about an old man whose manner of looking at life was entirely different from that of others in the village. We could all learn something from his philosophy.

It seems this old man had only one horse, and one day it ran away. His neighbors came and commiserated with him, telling him how sorry they were for the misfortune that had befallen him.

His answer surprised them. "But how do you know it's bad?" he asked.

A few days later his horse came back, and with it were two wild horses. Now the old man had three horses, when before he had only one. This time the neighbors congratulated him upon his good fortune.

"But how do you know it's good?" he replied.

The next day, while attempting to break in one of the wild horses, his son fell off and broke his leg. Once again the friendly neighbors came, this time to console the old man for the bad luck that had befallen his son.

"But how do you know it's bad?" he questioned. By this time the neighbors decided his mind was addled and didn't want to have any more to do with him.

However, the next day a warlord came through the village and took all the able-bodied young men off to war. But not the old man's son, because he was not able-bodied!

In this story one event follows another very quickly in order to make the point. In real life a great span of time may lapse between the happenings, which makes it more difficult to tie them together.

Regardless of this, we would all lead more serene lives if we were not so quick to pass judgement on the events as they occur. Even that which you resent the most, and which still causes a negative reaction when it comes to mind, may have played a positive part in your life.

Perhaps in looking back you will see that it was exactly the experience you needed to further your development. It helped make you the well-rounded person you are now. Without that particular experience, which you have resented for so long, you would not have gained the understanding and compassion you now possess.

Now, because of your increased knowledge and growth, you are ready for whatever wonderful new experiences are in store for you.

The great Roman emperor and philosopher Marcus Aurelius said, "Nothing happens to anyone which he is not formed by nature to bear."

Therefore, on Thanksgiving Day — and everyday —
"In everything give thanks." More often than not, future
events will prove your faith was justified.

45

Seek Inner Security

One of my recent articles on the subject of being thankful without prejudging brought an unusual amount of mail. Many expressed the belief that they would be better able to face whatever each day brings now they realize many experiences which appear at the time to be "bad" may turn out later to be "good."

One person, however, questioned the possibility of being thankful for some things, such as the incident in Guyana.

This is admittedly difficult to do. It is well-nigh impossible for rational people to express thanks for so many taking their own lives and the lives of their children.

On the other hand, this unfortunate incident might be instrumental in preventing thousands of others from looking outside of themselves for security. Those who are insecure and lack confidence and self-esteem will naturally be drawn to groups and leaders who seem to offer that for which they are so desperately searching.

This is not intended to infer that all groups or all "spiritual leaders" are harmful. In many cases they play a very helpful role. The danger lies in one's losing his individuality and thus his innate ability to think for himself. Then when an emergency or crisis erupts, all he is able to do is follow along with the crowd.

A sense of insecurity seems to be permeating our society to an ever-increasing degree. Many do not know what to believe in any more, and as a result they believe in little or nothing. This creates a vacuum — which nature abhors.

Now the possibility is opened up that one may be attracted to an undesirable source for something in which to believe. (An undesirable source is any source that prohibits one from thinking for himself, regardless of the good intentions of the group or its leader.)

One of the definitions of security is peace of mind. Peace of mind does not come easily. It may be necessary to put forth much effort to attain it. One method is to attempt to become as proficient as possible in the most important areas of your life.

Most of us face many different and sometimes adverse situations in the course of the day, week or month. Some of these situations are relatively inconsequential and should be regarded as such. For example, if your golf or tennis game is off it shouldn't cause you to feel insecure, unless you were a professional. In this case it would be important and you would take steps to correct your mistakes.

There are other situations that are vital to your peace of mind. If you are working, your job is a prime example. If you feel insecure in your job it is probably because you are not doing your best. This is within your own power to correct.

It is much easier to blame some other factor or person, but, unfortunately, that is not where the fault usually lies.

The same principle applies to a marriage. Those who are insecure in their marriage blame their feeling of insecurity on the other partner. "Why must you act this way?" "Why can't you be like other men (or other women)?"

If the insecure person would concentrate on improving himself, the relationship would improve and the uncertainty and insecurity would probably vanish of its own accord.

Every area of your life is within your province to improve, including your financial condition and your health. Your inner security and peace of mind will grow accordingly.

When faced with a problem, ask yourself, "What can I do to improve this situation without outside help?" When you have done all you can, you will find that very little outside help will be necessary. If you still feel you must seek help from another, be sure you seek it from someone who has overcome his or her own problems!

Concentrate on improving your abilities in the areas of your life that you will have to deal with most often. You will then feel secure because you are in control. Unhappiness and insecurity are the result of not being capable of handling situations as they occur.

Learn to rely on your God-given inner strength, rather than on another human being. Humans are fallible. Your own inner strength will see you through any situation you are called upon to face.

"The Lord does not change situations. He changes people and people change situations."

46

Let It Begin With Me

When violence strikes in our society and death and suffering result, no one completely escapes responsibility. We are all involved to some extent.

More than 300 years ago, author John Donne wrote: "No man is an island, entire of itself. Any man's death diminishes me, because I am involved in Mankind; and therefore never send to know for whom the bell tolls; it tolls for thee."

Each of us must take responsibility for the quality of life of the community in which we live. When an individual fails to take a stand and permissively allows perverse forces to infiltrate his environment, he must be held accountable for the resultant conditions.

Once these perverse forces gain a foothold, there is no turning them back unless everyone does become involved.

I once told the fable of the Arab and the camel. It was a cold night, and the camel begged the Arab at least to allow its head to seek comfort inside the tent. The Arab finally consented. It was only a matter of time until the camel had eased its entire body inside, and the Arab was outside!

The gradual lowering of moral standards was probably the forerunner of many of our current problems. It naturally followed that the fewer disciplinary measures were enforced, the lower the standards dropped.

The longest journey starts with a single step. The deterioration of a country, a city, or an individual starts when the general level of thought begins to decline. This happens so gradually it is scarcely noticed.

An unfailing indication that degeneracy is gaining a foothold is evident when one is no longer easily shocked. An example is the use of language that at one time would have been repulsive. Virtually all words become acceptable, and it isn't long before even the most prudish become immune. Pornographic books and movies inevitably follow and become an acceptable part of our culture.

It is not for me to judge whether things of this nature are either "good" or "bad." What I have done, however, is note the great changes that take place in individuals and communities when this degeneracy occurs.

In many phases of life it seems we are much more concerned with the effect than we are with the cause. If we have a headache or a toothache, we take a pain pill. The pain leaves temporarily, but the cause remains. People commit crimes and are removed from society. They come back, and the majority of them again commit crimes.

Whatever the reason or cause, it remains the same and will until the person himself changes inwardly. Little or nothing is done to bring about a change as we overlook the cause and deal with the effect.

The answer to a problem sometimes comes by looking backward. Observe the effects, or current conditions, and slowly trace past events until the cause is discovered.

Generally speaking, there seems to be a lack of genuine concern for others. This is not true of everyone, of course, but it is more prevalent than in previous generations. The basic cause may be the continuous population shift and the resulting feeling of impermanency.

In earlier times, families remained stationary to a much greater degree, giving everyone more sense of belonging. Now many feel as if they are living in a world full of strangers.

Instead of trusting one another, many have become fearful and suspicious. The words, "We live in a violent society," are constantly being repeated. Until this attitude is changed, we will continue to attract to our communities the very conditions we abhor the most.

It is within our power to raise the level of consciousness and change the quality of life in our environment. It won't happen, however, if we wait for someone else to do it.

As it has been said, "Let there be peace on earth, and let it begin with me."

47

Thoughts to Ponder

Some of the greatest wisdom is found in a single sentence or a solitary thought. A line or two expressing an idea is often more effective than many paragraphs.

I have been told that many of the old masters, being aware of the power of concentrated thought, used this method of teaching. They presented their students with a principle condensed into a sentence or two, then instructed them to meditate upon this one subject for an hour or more.

They apparently found that much greater understanding was gained this way than by more conventional methods of teaching.

Of course, life was probably lived at a much slower pace in those days and people had more patience. However, if you will take a principle that applies to a situation that is disturbing you and concentrate upon it, you will find it very beneficial.

It will give you a different perspective, and as your perspective changes regarding a situation the situation itself will change.

Here are some examples. (Unfortunately, when I save a line or quotation I sometimes neglect to save the name of the author or his or her profession. Hopefully, none of those still living will object to my use of their material. Usually the greater the person the more likely he will be willing to share his wisdom with others.)

None of the quotations are mine — only the comments. Here is one that applies to many people who have written to me complaining that someone is making them unhappy. This advice was given by philosopher Epictetus, who lived in the first and second centuries.

> "To permit another person to disturb your mental equilibrium is to offer yourself in slavery or, even worse, because a slave is one in body only, whereas you have made your soul servile to him. Any person capable of angering you becomes your master; he can anger you only when you permit yourself to be disturbed by him. We must not allow ourselves to become enslaved by anyone."

It is amazing to observe the changes that take place in those who gain this different perspective with regards to those with whom they are in constant disagreement. When they refuse to become angry, it usually isn't long before the other person stops acting in the manner that made them angry.

Many relationships would be improved immediately by following the advice of Epictetus. (Incidentally, I imagine that he would be surprised to know that his advice is being given 2,000 years after he first gave it.)

A modern writer and teacher, Raymond Barker, wrote:

> "We can do anything we wish if we will stop scattering our energy and organize our thinking.

Think of what you want, expect what you want and act as if you already had it.''

If you will observe your thoughts and actions objectively, you may find you have habitually done exactly the opposite. Most people seem to spend much more time dwelling upon the negative aspects of their lives than on the positive aspects.

How many times do you hear someone exclaim how wonderful he feels, compared to the number of times he tells you how badly he feels?

Please don't overlook Barker's last seven words. I have found from my own experience and that of many others that this is one of the greatest of the life-changing principles. In Mark 11:24 the Bible instructs us to demonstrate this example of complete faith and belief: *''Whatever you desire, pray believing you have already received it, and you shall have it.''*

Try acting as if you were already the person you aspire to be and see what happens.

Here is another quotation from an unknown author:

''New experiences do not come from looking backward, but from looking forward and upward.''

Many people live dull, uninteresting lives. They need new experiences but are afraid to seek them, perhaps because of past rejections or failures. Therefore, they are destined to remain unhappy and frustrated until and unless they realize that the past is over and only retains the power over them they choose to give it.

One way to motivate yourself to try something new is to ask yourself, "What is the worst thing that can happen to me should I fail?"

If you are truthful, you will invariably be forced to admit that even if you fail, you are no worse off than if you had never made the attempt.

Therefore, you have everything to gain and nothing to lose.

48

'Winning' Arguments

Years ago, I was called upon to serve on a jury. Although I served on only three cases, it was a great source of education. It is a fine way to learn about human nature and methods of handling people.

This is especially true in regard to those who are obnoxious and argumentative and unwilling to listen or recognize there might be another side to an issue.

The first case on which I served was extremely controversial. When both sides had presented their arguments and we were escorted into the jury room to arrive at a verdict, I began by being argumentative myself. I disagreed with most of the other jurors, but it didn't take me long to find that arguing with them would never convince them to change their opinions.

Of course the same situation exists outside of a jury room. It is virtually impossible to win an argument, and, if you do, you probably have lost a friend. No one likes to be proved wrong.

I discovered after much trial and error that it is best to allow others to prove themselves wrong. Thus, they cannot be offended with you, and it gives them a chance to save face.

In fact, if you are clever enough and kind enough, you can make it appear as though they agreed with you all the time. They might even believe this themselves.

There were some on each jury panel who were absolutely convinced they were right, even though they seldom had valid reasons for believing so. The less sure of themselves they were, the more they shouted. (This is almost always the case.) By accident, I discovered the method of handling this kind of person.

One man, named Art, had made up his mind almost before the trial began that the defendant was guilty. Only one other person besides myself did not share his opinion. As the trial progressed, I developed very valid reasons for believing in the man's innocence.

However, once in the jury room, I could see that my chances of convincing Art and the others were almost nil. Finally, I decided that instead of trying vainly to prove my point, I would ask Art to prove his.

"Excuse me," I said quietly, "please explain your reason for believing in the defendant's guilt. I am certainly willing to listen, because there is evidently some factor in the evidence that I completely overlooked."

"Anybody could tell he was guilty just by looking at him," he shouted. "Besides, he already had a criminal record."

"You're far too intelligent to believe that either of those reasons applies to this case," I answered. "Please give us the real reasons, from the evidence, you believe the man committed this particular crime."

"Well . . . well," he sputtered.

"We have plenty of time," I interjected. The poor fellow was making a fool of himself, and he knew it.

Finally his voice trailed off, and he sat down, to remain quiet the remainder of the session.

Then I asked the other jurors who had professed such a strong belief in the defendant's guilt to give their reasons. No one ventured a word, not wishing to be put in the same embarrassing position in which Art had placed himself. It was now easy for me to bring out the obvious discrepancies in the testimony, to which no one had apparently paid attention.

I suggested another vote. The first had been ten to two in favor of a guilty verdict. Now it was unanimous for acquittal. Subsequent events proved this verdict to be correct, as another man confessed to the crime.

The point of this story is not how to sway juries but rather how to avoid useless arguments. Simply ask the other person to state the reasons for his belief; then sit back quietly, without interrupting except to continue asking questions. Be sure you do not answer your own questions.

The other will probably become less certain of himself very soon. When he hesitates, intersperse your statement with an occasional, "Don't you agree?" or, "Don't you think so?"

You will find him nodding his head and grateful to you for permitting him to bow out gracefully, as if it were his opinion all along.

By using this method, you may be able to win an argument without losing a friend or making an enemy.

49

Limits Are Of Your Own Making

To permit others to place a label upon you and then to live up to that label, especially when it is against your nature, is foolish.

Even so, many persons do exactly this.

When you point out to them that they are acting in a certain manner because others expect them to do so, not because of their own choosing, it comes as a revelation.

There is a definite correlation between the way one acts and the way one is expected to act, not only by others but also by the person himself. Therefore, it is more effective to praise than to criticize.

Most of us live up to expectations, whether those of others or ourselves. For example, the rate of recidivism for ex-convicts is high because few expect them to go straight after their release. "Once a thief, always a thief," is a common expression, although not necessarily true.

Many end up in prison because the expectation of this was placed in their consciousness when they were young. Someone, perhaps a relative or teacher, had occasion to call the person a liar or thief or worthless. The person then proceeded, unconsciously at first, to act the part of a thief or liar or failure.

You may be leading a humdrum life, simply because that is what you have come to expect for yourself. This may be the result of your early environment and upbringing. You gradually assumed the characteristics which were imposed on you by others.

You may have assumed that the opinions of others, which influenced your own opinion of yourself, were correct. Begin now to question this assumption. Open your mind to the possibility that you might have greater potential than you have been led to believe.

Don't allow doubts or objections to pop up, such as, "I'm too old" or "too stupid," and so on. Eliminate such thoughts.

Picture yourself as having lived within an invisible circle surrounded by a fence, but now that fence suddenly disappears. Realize that all the beliefs you and others have held about you may have been entirely false. You cannot immediately change others' beliefs about you. As you change your own, theirs will change too.

For example, I worked many years ago for a company which sponsored a bowling team. One team consisted of five bowlers. So that the competition in the league would be as even as possible, each team was to consist of one top-notch bowler with an average of 180 or better, one almost as proficient, one about average, another with an average of 150, and a beginner who hopefully would average around 135.

Another fellow and I hadn't been bowling very long. We were almost equal in ability, or lack of it. However, one of us had to be placed in the 150-average category to conform to league rules. I was chosen for no other reason than that.

Strangely enough, I immediately considered myself a better bowler than my friend. When the league ended, my final average was 151, and his was 134. I had subsubconsciously accepted the fact that I was a 150 bowler, and he did the same with the 135 category.

Entire lives can be changed by changing inner beliefs about oneself. When you think about the past, concentrate on whatever successes you experienced. Do not dwell on the failures!

All the beliefs you hold which are based on the negative opinions of others are false and must be eliminated from your thoughts. As your beliefs about yourself become of a more positive nature, you will discover the limits you placed upon yourself were of your own making and do not really exist.

Your own mind is capable of removing all the blocks that stood in the way of a better, more rewarding life. The quality of your life is your responsibility.

50

Your Beliefs About Yourself are True

I received this question from a reader: "Why is so much importance attached to the way one believes? Something is either true or it is not true. Surely one's belief concerning it can't make any difference."

Many years ago, I began to realize that in order for a change for the better in a person's life to be permanent, a change must first take place in the person himself. Before that change can take place, I found, the person's beliefs concerning himself must change.

For example, if you remove a man from prison into society, it is only reasonable to assume he will commit the same acts that caused him to be incarcerated in the first place, unless a change has taken place within him.

Other examples are of persons who experience sudden wealth or unexpected success. Inwardly, they are still the same persons as when they were poor or considered failures. Their inner beliefs concerning themselves are unable to change to correspond to their new outer conditions. As a result, it will not be long before their outer conditions will change back to their original state.

Someone has said, "You will always find a way to prove that your beliefs about yourself are true." One's newfound wealth or success will be short-lived if one believes he doesn't deserve it.

I once knew a young man who was barely able to make ends meet financially. He had a wife and two children and was always hoping for the break that would provide his family with a decent home.

One day, he made the "killing" that is the ultimate dream of every gambler. First, he played the slot machine in Reno and hit the jackpot for $150. He then played blackjack and won $500 more. Next, he played dice and couldn't lose. After a few hours, he was $25,000 ahead.

He was drinking heavily by this time, and his friends literally dragged him away from the tables and put him to bed. He slept for a few hours, woke up, and sneaked out of his room and began playing again. By nightfall, he had to borrow bus fare home!

Stories such as this are fairly common. Through the years, this young man had developed the belief that he was a "loser," and this sudden good fortune could not change his thinking. He was bound to find a way for his outer circumstances to conform to his inner beliefs about himself, so he ended up broke.

Many believe that a change for the better in their lives is out of the question. This belief keeps them from trying. Therefore, it is their own beliefs that prevent any chance they may have had of effecting an improvement. They will never follow the priceless admonition of Ralph Waldo Emerson, the 19th century essayist and poet, "Do the thing and you will have the power." They don't believe it is possible.

It would be sad enough if it were only our own negative beliefs that affect our lives. Unfortunately, this is not true. We permit others' beliefs concerning our abilities to influence our actions. Why delegate all this power to another? You be the one to decide what your capabilities are and don't unconsciously limit yourself.

No one's life is "cut and dried" unless he believes it to be. A false belief such as this can be tragic. Many young persons end up in prison because of it.

I have talked with convicts who said they believe that the only way they would ever gain material possessions of any value would be to steal them. Their belief in this assumption caused it to be true so far as they were concerned, so they never made the effort to acquire possessions honestly. They never will, unless they change their beliefs about themselves.

I personally have seen many people effect dramatic changes in their lives by developing a better self-image. This experience has been very rewarding but it also makes me more aware of the many wasted lives that could have had more meaning. All it takes is the refusal to accept the limitations you and others have imposed upon you, and then you must take the first step. Don't allow what has happened in the past to determine your future.

Everyone has a great capacity for growth and expression, but if you cannot conceive of this, it will never materialize. A change in experience can happen only to a changed person.

About the Author

Doug Hooper is a rarity. With no previous background, he moved toward a career in writing and lecturing at the age of 58. Now, six years later, his newspaper column reaches two million homes and he is in great demand as a speaker.

When asked what happened to cause such a dramatic change, Doug says, "I changed my thinking about myself. I realized all my limits were false and were self-imposed. Then I was able to move out of the invisible circle in which I had been living all of my life."

Doug was born in Alameda, California in 1916. He was a salesman for over 40 years. In 1961, a series of events led him to conduct classes in California prisons on a voluntary basis. Dramatic changes took place in the lives of the convicts who applied the principles and Natural Laws of which Doug writes in this book.

He began to lecture on the subject, and when the editor of a local newspaper heard him, a weekly column resulted. Now Doug has many hundreds of letters from those who have experienced changes in their lives as a result of his writings. Fifty of these inspiring articles are contained in this book.